British Military *Greats*

British Military *Greats*

Introduction by Peter Snow

Edited by Annabel Merullo and Neil Wenborn

Contents

Introduction
Peter Snow

What is it that makes Britain's armed forces so special? The answer is in the pages of this book. Each of these essays tells the compelling story of one element in the kaleidoscope of people and events that makes up Britain's military history. It is a catalogue of triumph and tragedy, ingenuity, audacity and outstanding human achievement. Some of these stories are about individual people, from commanders like Montgomery and Marlborough to Florence Nightingale, Flora Sandes and winners of the Victoria Cross like Flight Lieutenant Eric Nicolson whose valour and humanity have given them a place in history. Others are about unique groups of people like the SAS, the Marines, the SOE, and the teams that invented the tank and the Spitfire. The names of the leaders, the tools of war and the times may have changed unrecognisably, but if there is one thing that binds these subjects together it is their greatness. These essays describe people and acts that have had a lasting and decisive impact on the country.

Britain has been forged on the battlefield. Not only were its constituent parts, Scotland, England and Wales, assembled by conquest, but the relatively recent birth of Britain itself was cemented and legitimised by constant warfare against continental foes. The victory over the Spanish Armada provided a foundation myth for Britain and her new empire. Subsequent wars against Spain and then France established a single, united nation. Redcoated Scottish Highlanders now stood shoulder to shoulder with men from Pembrokeshire, Cornwall and Kent on battlefields throughout the world.

But it was not always thus. Peoples have come to these islands to settle or conquer from all over Europe. It is an essential attribute of Britishness that we are inheritors of not one but several military traditions. The warlike Celts, the axe-wielding Anglo-Saxons, the ferocious Scots and the Welsh longbowmen all have their place in the following pages. As modern Britons we are heirs to them all.

One of the surprising things about the essays is what they tell us about Britishness. It is often claimed that we British love nothing more than a plucky hero, doomed to fail. There are, to be sure, moments of suicidal bravery and glorious defeat. Boudicca and Lord Cardigan have seen to that. But what comes across very strongly are some entirely different British attributes which receive a lot less attention. We were supposedly a class-ridden, hierarchical society, and yet the majority of the commanders in the book had fairly humble backgrounds. And all of them, whether they were kings, aristocrats or commoners, were loved by the soldiers they led.

Similarly, Britain is now not usually associated with the rapid advancement of science. Yet the British have introduced new technology to the battlefield as no other nation has. The longbow, the 'race-built' Elizabethan galleons, the Dreadnought and radar all revolutionised the way that wars were fought. These innovations were the result of inspired leadership, military and civilian cooperation, and determination not to be imprisoned by conventional wisdom.

These British military greats do not exude 'effortless superiority'. Far from it. All the successes in this book are hard won. Andrew Roberts demonstrates Churchill's startling attention to detail in the preparation of his 1940 speeches. They were the result of a lifetime of careful planning and rehearsals in front of mirrors. This professionalism, says Len Deighton, was the chief strength of Park and Dowding in the Battle of Britain. Dowding is almost an anti-British stereotype: introverted and uncharismatic but a brilliant commander in the battle with the Luftwaffe. Again, the bombing of the Ruhr dams was an operation that took years to plan and required huge innovation. John Sweetman's description of Operation Chastise gives a balanced view of that extraordinary raid which did so much to boost British morale. The breaking of the Enigma code, too, was the work of an eccentric bunch of mathematicians whose tireless efforts, Hugh Sebag-Montefiore suggests, may have shortened the war by one to two years.

Wars are won by the brilliant strategist and the footslogging soldier at the sharp end. Britain has been fortunate to have plenty of quality in both departments. The essays reflect that. Robert Hardy on the Welsh and English longbowmen at Agincourt, Gary Sheffield's description of 'the Redcoat', Julian Thompson on the Royal Marines, all do justice to men whose names and faces may be largely lost to us now but whose courage, discipline and skill won victories around the globe. From Finland to South Africa, from China to the Caribbean, British soldiers, sailors and airmen lie in foreign graves.

The men who led them are perhaps better remembered, and an élite amongst them appear throughout the book. Alfred the Great, Robert the Bruce, Cromwell, Marlborough, Wolfe, Slim – it is a roll call of great commanders. Each essay teases out a particular quality. Charles Spencer points to Marlborough's determination to bring overwhelming force to bear on one point of the enemy's front line. Julian Thompson illustrates Slim's good humour and optimism in the face of apparent disaster. Viscount Montgomery of Alamein was a meticulous planner, as was the Duke of Wellington. The Iron Duke and Sir Francis Drake, as Jane Wellesley and John Elliot show, had the ability to project a sense of calm in moments of great crisis. The former gave the signal for action only after seeing out the Duchess of Richmond's ball and the latter after finishing his game of bowls.

Len Deighton points out that we British have a healthy disrespect for uniforms. We are not a militaristic people and have always shown a cheerful scepticism towards our army in particular. Today Britain's armed forces are small. But they have an outstanding reputation for military skill and restraint: massively reduced in number though they are, they are as busy as ever. They, more than any other arm of government, are what allows Britain to punch above its weight. A British soldier has been killed in action every year since World War II except for 1968. The great tradition of professionalism, courage and duty which this book celebrates, from the Iron Age warrior to today's Special Forces, is as relevant now as it has ever been.

The flying aces of World War I
Patrick Bishop

On 25 August 1914, three weeks into the Great War, Lieutenant C. E. C. Rabagliati of the Royal Flying Corps was cruising with an observer on a reconnaissance mission over northern France when they came across a lone German aeroplane. Rabagliati's aircraft was unarmed, but he had with him a .303 service rifle. The German carried a Mauser pistol fitted with a wooden shoulder stock. The two machines approached each other and circled, coming within yards of colliding. Rabagliati fired 100 rounds without success. Then, he later reported, 'to my intense joy I saw the German pilot fall forward on his joystick and the machine tipped up and went down'.

Such encounters were to be repeated thousands of times in the following years as aeroplanes became an increasingly important element in the armouries of the rival armies. The rickety wood and canvas constructions lifted the roof off the battlefield, allowing commanders to glimpse the enemy's territory, detect his dispositions and movements, and inform their guess as to his intentions. They were further used to spot the fall of shot during the artillery bombardments that took up so much of the military effort, and to signal corrections.

The undesirability of allowing hostile aircraft over one's territory meant that the business of shooting down the enemy became an end in itself. This was what fighter pilots did, and it was this aspect of the work of the RFC which became best known to the British public as they followed, with dread and fascination, the progress of the war in their morning newspapers.

Fighter planes and the men who flew them played a relatively minor part in settling the outcome of the war. Yet their activities attracted wide attention. They were a godsend to propagandists desperate to find some romance amid the horror of mechanised warfare. They operated in the clean medium of the air, detached from the vileness of the trenches. The nature of their work made it inevitable that they would be linked to an older, nobler fighting tradition. Some aviators believed this themselves, at least at the beginning. 'To be alone,' wrote Cecil Lewis, who flew with the RFC over the Western Front, 'to have your life in your own hands, to use your own skill, single-handed against the enemy. It was like the lists in the Middle Ages, the only sphere in modern warfare where a man saw his adversary and faced him in mortal combat, the only sphere where there was still chivalry and honour.'

The propagandists' work was helped by the rich quality of the material they had to work with. Flying attracted extraordinary people: independent-minded, adventurous and unconventional, often to the point of eccentricity.

Among the first to emerge was Albert Ball, in whom the values of the playing field jostled unhappily with the neuroses of the battlefield. Ball was brought up in a middle-class home in Nottingham where his father hauled himself up the class ladder, starting his

Heir to an older tradition of chivalry: Albert Ball of the Royal Flying Corps

working life as a plumber and ending up mayor of the city. He was educated at a local fee-paying school founded to promote Anglican principles and a sense of patriotic duty. There were cold baths, perpetual exercise and an emphasis on technology.

He joined up as soon as war broke out and, frustrated at the delay in being sent to the front, took flying lessons to improve his chances of getting into the RFC. Ball fell instantly in love with flying, despite the hazards. 'It is rotten to see the smashes,' he wrote in one of his frequent letters home. 'Yesterday a ripping boy had a smash and when we got to him he was nearly dead. He had a two inch piece of wood right through his head and died this morning.'

He arrived in France in time for the great Somme offensive, and distinguished himself immediately. In his French Nieuport, one of the new generation of single-seater fighters, he flew straight into packs of German aircraft, getting in close, firing his Lewis machine gun at point-blank range, breaking off only when his ammunition was exhausted. It was effective but terribly risky. He would return from sorties with his aeroplane in tatters.

Even in the highly individualistic milieu of the RFC Ball struck his fellow aviators as odd. At his first air base, Savy Aubigny near Arras, he turned down a billet in the village and lived in a tent, growing his own vegetables. In the evening he avoided the mess, preferring to play his violin. A famous photograph of Ball shows a boyish figure with taut, unlined skin, thick glossy hair and a bland, unreadable expression. But there was turmoil behind the calm exterior. Almost from the beginning the mild bragging in the letters home is matched by disgust at what he was doing. Within a few months of arriving in France he was yearning for home. 'I do so want to leave all this beastly killing for a time,' he wrote. Yet even when complaining of nerves, he would still take every possible opportunity to get airborne.

When he was finally ordered back to England in October 1916 for a rest and to take up an instructing post, his record as the most effective pilot in the RFC had made him a national figure. The Prime Minister, Lloyd George, invited him to breakfast. He went to Buckingham Palace, where King George V presented him with the MC and DSO.

Ball soon grew unhappy with his cushy billet and was agitating to return to the front. In February he was posted to 56 Squadron, which was being formed near London. While waiting to leave for France, he met an 18-year-old florist, Flora Young, and fell in love. His tour was meant to be only for a month. Once he had overtaken the record set by the German ace Oswald Boelcke, he wrote to her, he would come home. On the afternoon of Monday 7 May 1917 he led a squadron of SE5s on an offensive sweep. He disappeared into a cloud and emerged flying upside down and trailing black smoke to crash into a hillside.

By the time of Ball's death another hero was emerging from the ranks of the RFC, a man of very different background and character. Edward 'Mick' Mannock was 27, the son of a violent-tempered Irish NCO who served with the Second Inniskilling Dragoons. The hardship of his early life converted him to socialism, and his Celtic roots made him a fervent Irish nationalist, all of which resulted in some lively discussions in the mess. He was a natural pilot and a bundle of contradictions. His diary mixes vindictiveness with bouts of remorse. He seemed genuinely to enjoy air fighting, writing about it as 'fun' and 'sport' in the manner of the times. One day he is recording how he let a German have 60 rounds at ten yards range 'so there wasn't much left of him … rough luck but it's war and they're Huns'. On another, after shooting down an enemy in flames, he records that it was 'a horrible sight and made me feel sick'.

Mannock was obsessed with the prospect of dying a fiery death in a 'flamerino'. He carried a revolver in the cockpit 'to finish myself at the first sign of flames'. On leave in London in June 1918, he fell ill with influenza and spent several days in bed in the RFC Club, unable to sleep because of the nightmares of burning aircraft that swamped him every time he closed his eyes. The following month he was dead, shot down, apparently, from the ground. His aeroplane erupted in flames as it crashed. At the time of his death he was credited with shooting down 74 German aircraft, against Ball's total of 43.

In many ways the pair were untypical of the general run of RFC pilots. Ball was teetotal and had no girlfriend until his meeting with Flora. Mannock drank little and seems to have shown a courtly restraint towards females. The ethos of the RFC was public-school, overlaid with a stylish raffishness that evoked an early 19th-century cavalry regiment. The pilots tended to like women, who were in abundant supply in the brothels and cafés of Amiens and Arras. They also often drank heavily, trying to blot out the memory of what had happened and what lay ahead.

The pilots' contribution to the war effort was made at a heavy cost in lives. But if the role they played in the victory was peripheral, their actions stood out against the muddy slaughter of the trenches and enthused a generation of boys who read of their exploits in comic books and the Biggles novels of W. E. Johns, himself a former RFC pilot. Twenty-two years after the end of the war a new generation of fighter pilots would be called upon to fight a really decisive battle, on which the future of the free world depended. For many, if not most, of the British pilots flying in the Battle of Britain, it was the example of aces like Ball and Mannock which had been their initial inspiration.

Alfred the Great
Max Adams

At Easter AD 878 Alfred, king of the West Saxons, could claim lordship over no more than a few square miles of Somerset marsh. The kingdoms of Northumbria, East Anglia and Mercia, and now the whole south of England, had been invaded and brought to submission by the *micel here*, the 'Great Host' of the Danish Vikings. By the time Alfred's grandson Athelstan died two generations later, all England south of the Humber was united in one kingdom, and the whole of the islands of Britain recognised his overlordship.

England is Alfred's legacy. His military and administrative triumphs stand alone in British history, and they are all the more remarkable for the circumstances in which he achieved them. Like Charlemagne before him, and perhaps only Napoleon afterwards, he had the vision to build the foundations for a political and social entity whose fruits could only possibly be reaped long after his own death.

Alfred was born at Wantage in AD 849, the fifth son of Aethelwulf, king of the West Saxons. Wessex was potentially the wealthiest of the Anglo-Saxon kingdoms, with rich forests, downland and fertile soils; but its long coast made it vulnerable to attack by sea, and it had traditionally been a wary rival of Mercia. Like its neighbours, it had long maintained relations with the European continent, and Aethelwulf, perhaps more naturally a cleric than a king, had an especially international outlook. In 853 he sent the four-year-old Alfred to Rome, and two years later he himself made the political and spiritual pilgrimage, taking his youngest son with him. So Alfred had twice visited many of the courts of the European kings before he was seven years old; a later admiring Pope sent him a fragment of the true cross.

Alfred can have had no expectation of becoming king. However, one by one, between Aethelwulf's death in 858 and his own accession in 871, all his older brothers died. Peculiarly for the early medieval period, none of them died in battle. One must suspect a physiological family weakness; Alfred himself was ill for much of his life. He suffered terribly from piles, according to his biographer Asser, and another mysterious illness that crippled him with pain – it may have been a stress-induced bowel complaint or a family predisposition to stomach cancer.

In any case, he inherited a kingdom at war. In the autumn of 865 the Great Host landed in East Anglia under their kings Ivar Boneless, Halfdan and the sons of Ragnar Lothbrook. Previous raids over three-quarters of a century had been just that: war bands plundering for treasure and ransom. This army was different. It was bent on conquest.

Its tactics were simple. The Danes would seize a defensible site, moving rapidly up navigable rivers in their longboats and then along Roman roads and ancient trackways in groups of mounted warriors. They would fortify the chosen site, ravage its hinterland, and

His victories laid the foundations of a united England: a 19th-century portrait of Alfred the Great

sell peace to those who could afford it. In this way they took York in 867, Mercia in 868 and East Anglia in 869.

In 870 it was the turn of Wessex. The Great Host, numbering perhaps 10,000 men, wintered at Reading. In January 871 they were confronted at Ashdown in Berkshire by the West Saxon army under King Aethelred and his younger brother Alfred, still only 21 years old. The Danes fled, but within a fortnight had regrouped and defeated the West Saxons. Then in April Aethelred died, leaving Alfred to fight nine more engagements through that year. At the end of the campaigning season his army was exhausted and he was forced to sue for peace.

The military infrastructure inherited by Alfred was simply inadequate to deal with the speed and mobility of his enemies. Its basis was three levels of obligation. Individual lords, or *thegns*, kept personal retinues. These bands of warriors, mostly mounted, would undertake engagements on their lord's initiative. These might be against neighbouring *thegns* in a land dispute, or the result of a blood-feud, or to defend their land against Viking or Mercian attack. At the shire level ealdormen were required to raise a *fyrd*, consisting of the bands of individual *thegns* and others who owed military service. At a national level there was the host, or *folc*, led by the king himself.

The extent to which a king could mobilise the entire national host depended on his personal authority and the political interests of his ealdormen and *thegns*. The speed with which they might take the field was quite another thing. Communication was difficult, and in mustering his army Alfred faced an understandable reluctance on the part of many warriors to leave home. Furthermore, an entire year's campaigning, such as Alfred undertook in 871 (and several times thereafter), put an intolerable strain on men who were needed for harvesting and ploughing and looking to the defence of their own families. Anglo-Saxon armies sometimes just decided to go home. And like a firefighter, Alfred might find himself chasing one enemy army while another landed 200 miles away. So while he was in the field, he must also look to a long-term restructuring of the national defences.

Alfred had a respite of a few years from major Viking attacks. He used this time to reinforce his personal authority and to gain a deep insight into his kingdom. He must have been constantly on the move, from Devon in the west to Kent in the east, using his personal wealth and influence to bind *thegns* to him, and gaining an intimate knowledge of the complex geography of the kingdom.

In 875 a large part of the Great Host, under King Guthrum, made another attempt to conquer Wessex. Alfred's army fought several more engagements, most of them indecisive. Such indecision was a feature of early medieval warfare, in which warriors rode to the battlefield, dismounted and formed a close shield-wall to advance on the enemy in a straight fight. Victory went to the holder of the battlefield, but a defeated enemy seems to have been able to reform quickly to fight another engagement. 'Great slaughter' is often described by the chroniclers; in reality, it must have been the exception.

This pattern of desultory pitched battle was broken in the second week of January 878, when Guthrum's army made a lightning advance from Gloucester and descended upon Chippenham with devastating effect. Alfred's fragile kingdom seems almost to have collapsed overnight. He fled, with a small personal retinue, to the safety of Athelney in the Somerset marshes, and mounted a series of guerrilla raids on Guthrum's army while he attempted to regroup his forces. By May, astonishingly, Alfred had gathered sufficient forces from across the south-west to mount a massive counterattack against the Danes, defeating them decisively at Edington in Wiltshire and forcing such punitive terms on Guthrum that he submitted to being baptised and withdrew his army to East Anglia.

From this point on Alfred's strategy was offensive. He captured and garrisoned London, and was recognised as overlord by all Englishmen outside Danish territories. He began to fight naval actions against Danish raiders, and embarked on a massive shipbuilding programme. He then planned and began to implement his greatest achievement, the network of 30 defended towns and forts across southern England that would ensure no part of the kingdom was more than a day's march from one of them. He chose their sites brilliantly: river crossings, nodes of Roman road networks, ancient hillforts commanding high ground. Only one was ever captured, and that when it was half-built. Alfred now had the crucial advantage of defensible bases from which to launch rapid counterattacks.

He then began reforming his military structure, bullying and cajoling a recalcitrant Saxon nobility into agreement, so that only half of his forces would ever be in the field at one time: it was the first English standing army. He innovated tactically too: aiming to cut the enemy from its supply chain, capturing their ships, and constructing double-forts to guard both sides of the major rivers. As he foresaw, by the end of his reign Wessex had become the least attractive place for the armies of the Vikings to attack, and they turned their attentions to the Continent. Alfred had overcome the most feared military force of the age.

After Alfred's death in 899, his children Edward the Elder and Aethelflaed built on these achievements to reconquer England below the Humber, and ensured the beginnings of English nationalism. For Alfred, rightly recognised as the greatest of the English kings, military success was an essential means to a more important end: the instigation of a moral, religious and educational framework that survives as the basis of English society.

The defeat of the Spanish Armada
John Elliott

Great victories – and great defeats, too – sometimes become defining events in the shaping of a nation's image of itself. So it was with the defeat of the Invincible Armada. The Spanish galleons moving in stately formation up the Channel for their rendezvous with the Duke of Parma's army; Sir Francis Drake finishing his game of bowls on Plymouth Hoe; the fireships wreaking havoc among the vessels anchored off Calais; Elizabeth's speech to the troops at Tilbury; and the storm that dispersed the great ships and littered the shores of Ireland with the wrecks of the defeated Armada as it limped home to Spain – these scenes were replayed in the nation's collective consciousness for generation after generation, and helped keep alive the memory of 1588 as a providential year in English history.

'The magnitude of the catastrophe,' wrote James Anthony Froude nearly three centuries later, 'took possession of the nation's imagination.' Yet at the time, many weeks were to pass before the scale of the disaster that had overtaken the Spanish fleet came to be realised. Although a sermon was preached at St Paul's on 20 August, praising God 'for our great victory by Him given to the English nation', no major public thanksgiving was ordered until late November, when it was timed to coincide with the 30th anniversary of the Queen's accession. There followed a week of services, sermons and processions, with lighting of bonfires and ringing of bells. The theme was deliverance: God had delivered His chosen people in their hour of need. This was, first and foremost, a great religious event, offering indisputable proof that God was Protestant. Medals were struck in England and the rebel provinces of the Netherlands, showing the ships of the Armada being dispersed by the 'Protestant' wind, along with appropriate inscriptions: 'He blew and they were scattered.' The Armada proclaimed the triumph, through divine intervention, of the international Protestant cause over the Antichrist in Rome and his wicked instrument, the King of Spain.

As it happens, the events of the next few years were to show that, at least in the short run, the victory over the Spaniards was not quite as conclusive as it must have seemed in that exhilarating autumn of 1588. Within two or three years, the Spain of Philip II was looking at least as formidable as when the Armada first set sail, and its naval recovery was sufficiently rapid for Philip to be able to order the despatch of fresh expeditions against the British Isles in 1596 and 1597, only to see them dispersed again by storms. The threat of successful invasion had now effectively passed, and with hindsight it can be seen that the Protestant cause was safe, but well into the 17th century the continent still lived under the shadow of Spain, with all the silver of America at its command.

Yet perceptions count for at least as much as realities in the shaping of national consciousness. This was true of Spain and England alike. For Spain, the defeat of the

The Armada Portrait *painted to celebrate Elizabeth's success against the Spanish*

'Enterprise of England' came as a devastating shock. When a nation thinks of itself as specially chosen for some divine purpose, failure is hard to understand. God, it seemed, had turned against it, and the best explanation for this sudden loss of divine favour seemed to be collective sinfulness. The incipient psychology of failure would be reinforced in succeeding decades by each new reverse to Spanish arms. In England, by contrast, the defeat of the Armada was to prove a crucial element in the eventual construction of a psychology of success.

Although no special day was set aside for the annual commemoration of the great victory of 1588, celebrations of the events of that fateful year were to be subsumed after 1605 into a wider national celebration, held each November, for a second act of divine deliverance – the discovery of the Gunpowder Plot. November was also the month in which Elizabeth, of happy memory, had come to the throne. During difficult times in the 17th century, when it seemed that Protestantism and liberty were again in mortal danger from the forces of popery, the recollection of the great queen, of the defeat of the Armada and of the uncovering of the villainy of Guy Fawkes provided comforting reassurance of the mercy that could be expected for the nation if it remained faithful to its God. Then, by a supreme act of providence, just 100 years after the defeat of the Armada, the nation was again delivered out of deadly peril when William of Orange disembarked at Torbay on 5 November 1688, and a Glorious Revolution ensured the triumph of liberty and Protestantism alike.

By the early 18th century, all the essential elements of England's national self-image were in place – a country that, against overwhelming odds, had seen off its enemies, first the Spaniards, then the French, and was both Protestant and free. The triumphs of the following two centuries – command of the seas, the acquisition of empire, and global dominance – only served to confirm the verdict of 1588, and reinforced the message of a divinely appointed national destiny for England and its peoples (generously embracing the Scots, the Welsh and the Irish, or at least those of Protestant descent).

Until the 19th century the public commemoration of centenaries was unusual, and it was not until 1888 that an attempt was made to organise a centenary celebration of 1588. An appeal was launched at the Mansion House for a national memorial to be erected on Plymouth Hoe, and a rather indiscriminate exhibition of Armada mementoes was put on display at the Plymouth Guildhall. But this was essentially a West Country initiative, and at the national level the commemorations seem to have fallen rather flat. The triumph of liberty and Protestantism was now taken for granted, and Britannia ruled the waves.

Ironically, it was only in 1988, when England's global dominance had long since passed, and the national identity itself was coming to be called into question, that an exhibition was mounted which recalled the events of 1588 on an appropriately epic scale. To the expression of considerable indignation in some quarters, scrupulous care was taken at the National Maritime Museum to give the Spanish side of the story equal weight to the English. Where were the heroes of yesteryear? No longer central to the national mythology, the defeat of the Armada had disappeared from the realm of the transcendental to become one more spectacular historical event.

The Battle of Britain
Len Deighton

By July 1940 Hitler's victorious fighting forces faced Britain all round the continental coast. Logic suggested that Britain should negotiate a surrender, but the British have never been noted for their logic. Inspired by Prime Minister Winston Churchill, virtually the whole nation were determined to continue the war.

The ensuing battle to establish air supremacy preparatory to a full-scale German invasion lasted for several weeks during the summer of 1940. After attacking coastal convoys in the English Channel, the German air force made daylight bombing raids on towns, ports, RAF airfields and other chosen targets across south-east England.

The pilots defending England against the German bomber fleets are usually remembered as middle-class young officers from public schools. It is tempting to compare them with the subalterns who served in the trenches in World War I, their sensitivity and sacrifice recorded in the poetry and prose of that war. In fact, the world had changed. About a quarter of the 1940 fighter pilots were sergeants. Of these about two-fifths were peacetime civilians who had joined the volunteer reserve and attended local flying-schools at government expense. Other part-time flyers had spent their weekends with the fully equipped Auxiliary Air Force squadrons. Of the RAF's peacetime sergeant pilots, many had been picked from the RAF schools for young trade apprentices. No less important were the Australians, New Zealanders, Canadians and South Africans, as well as highly motivated professional pilots from the air forces of the occupied nations. A Czech pilot is usually credited with the highest number of victories during the Battle of Britain.

Commanding RAF Fighter Command was Air Chief Marshal Sir Hugh 'Stuffy' Dowding, a shy and lonely workaholic. His loyal right-hand man was Air Vice-Marshall Keith Park, an ace of World War I, who commanded all the fighter units in south-east England, the battle area. These were men untrammelled by conventional military thinking (and who were ignominiously repaid after the victory by subjection to an enquiry and replacement by rivals; even today, despite the energetic work of the redoubtable Bill Bond and the Battle of Britain Historical Society, the men in Whitehall and Westminster resolutely oppose the creation of a proper memorial to the people who fought the battle).

Vitally important to the victory was Lord Beaverbrook, the maverick press tycoon Churchill had appointed to rectify the bureaucratic bumbling that crippled the aircraft industry. Breaking rules, and assuming powers he was never granted, the 'Beaver' was rich enough and influential enough openly to defy the civil servants, the industrialists and the bomber barons. He concentrated upon building fighter aircraft as quickly as possible and speedily repairing those that were damaged – a success for which his enemies never forgave him.

Overleaf: *RAF pilots scramble for action during the Battle of Britain*

The Messerschmitt Bf 109E and the Spitfire were about evenly matched in performance and effectiveness (the superiority of the Spitfire came later with the development of the Rolls-Royce Merlin 60 series engines). But most of the RAF single-seat fighters were Hawker Hurricanes. Heavier, slower and less sophisticated, the Hurricanes were, whenever possible, sent to attack the bombers rather than face the Bf 109s. All these aircraft had fuel enough for about one and a half hours of flying. Despite using grass airfields very near the coast, the Germans had only a brief time over England; the RAF also had to fight while watching their fuel gauges.

The RAF radar of the period was a simple device that bounced a transmitted signal off an approaching aircraft. By measuring its return, the position of the enemy could be estimated. Most of the tall radar masts along the British coast gave an approximate range and rough estimate of height and direction. To fix an enemy's position, the RAF plotters measured the ranges given by two neighbouring stations and noted the place where they intersected.

As well as having supervised the development of Britain's radar, Dowding had created Britain's unique reporting network. A 'filter room' and many 'operations rooms' processed the reports from the radar stations. The 'plotters' – young servicewomen – used croupiers' rakes to shove brightly coloured counters across the map tables. These constantly moving chips were marked to represent the enemy bombers, the enemy fighters and the RAF defenders. 'Tote boards' on the wall lit up to show local RAF fighter squadrons and the degree of their readiness (how many aircraft were in the air, how many being refuelled and rearmed, how many damaged, how many lost). Often the Germans would launch several raids at once, or a feint to draw the RAF into the air before the time of a major attack. Sitting in a glass-fronted balcony above the plot, a 'controller' watched the raids develop in his area and decided when to 'scramble' which squadrons into the air for maximum advantage. By talking to the pilots he could guide them to an interception. In what must remain a miracle of efficiency, the map tables were seldom more than four minutes – about 15 miles – behind events.

The world had never known an engagement like this. Height was the trump card in this sort of conflict. Here was a battlefield in three dimensions – four if the vital factor of time is included. Crowds gathered in city streets and outside village pubs to watch the fleets of bombing planes and their escorts; and the RAF climbing, climbing, climbing to intercept. And watched them tumbling down to earth.

By the middle of September even the most optimistic of the Luftwaffe leaders were admitting that there was no chance of subduing the RAF fighter opposition in time for an invasion. Both sides were becoming exhausted. German flyers returned to report that there were still plenty of RAF fighters coming up to meet them. The days grew shorter, and storms and fogs and rough seas would soon come. Revisionist historians sometimes claim that the Battle of Britain decided nothing; that the Royal Navy would have protected Britain against German invasion. This idea cannot be sustained when considering the fate of warships within range of heavy bombers.

As September ended, the invasion schemes had been put back into the plans chests and the German sailors breathed a sigh of relief. Hitler turned his attention to the Soviet Union, and the Luftwaffe to the less challenging task of bombing London by night.

In 1940 the victories of Germany's highly professional armed forces had brought a great measure of overconfidence to all concerned. Civilian ideas, and even those of scientists, tended to be overruled in favour of traditional German military methods. Even within the Wehrmacht, technicians, such as intelligence officers and logistics experts, were given low ranks and meagre resources, and found it difficult to influence the decisions of high command. In 1940 German intelligence knew very little about British defences. For example, attacks upon radar towers (tall masts impossible to conceal or camouflage) were abandoned because Luftwaffe planners had no idea of the vital role they played in Dowding's reporting network.

The British prevailed because their armed forces remained essentially civilian in mentality. Scientists, many of whom had already worked with the RAF to create the radar network, were welcomed into RAF meetings and messes. Everyone acknowledged that the telephone engineers, repairing lines during bombing raids, were vital participants in the battle. Lord Beaverbrook may have been the most unruly of civilians, but he became one of Dowding's closest associates.

Britain won because the British retained a healthy mistrust of uniforms and authority; and this extended even to those who wore the uniforms and had the authority. Long may it be so.

The sinking of the Bismarck
Andrew Lambert

In May 1941 Britain stood alone, facing the might of Nazi Germany and Fascist Italy. Her only military support came from the Dominions and the Empire; her only allies were the truncated exile forces of conquered Europe. Among the neutrals, only the United States was supporting Britain, providing arms, loans and limited naval patrols.

While the threat of a German invasion had been crushed by British naval power and the Royal Air Force, Britain depended on her oceanic lifelines for food, weapons and manpower. If she could not use the sea she would be forced to surrender. The vital North Atlantic sea lanes linked Canada, the United States and their resources with Britain. From the opening day of the war this shipping had been convoyed in close ordered formations of 20 to 30 ships escorted by destroyers, sloops and corvettes. The principal threat came from German submarines – U-boats – occasional Luftwaffe sorties and a handful of powerful surface warships. While the Germans had sunk millions of tons of merchant shipping by May 1941, they had not compromised the convoy system. The supplies still got through.

However, Grand Admiral Erich Raeder believed he had the answer. A powerful surface force in the Atlantic could annihilate slow-moving convoys and their anti-submarine escorts. He would place the British on the horns of a dilemma. Unable to provide every convoy with a battleship, they would be forced to disperse the merchant ships, which would then be slaughtered by U-boats. Earlier warship sorties had been successful, but they had avoided British battleships. Raeder knew that the focus of German efforts was about to shift east: Operation Barbarossa would unleash a massive invasion of the Soviet Union in June. The German navy had one last chance to affect the outcome of the war. The brand new super-battleship *Bismarck*, a 45,000-ton monster armed with eight 15-inch guns and capable of 30 knots, could destroy the convoy system. With the Soviet Union being overrun, the British might surrender. Accompanied by the heavy cruiser *Prinz Eugen*, and supported by eight pre-positioned supply ships, the *Bismarck* would challenge British control of the Atlantic.

However, Raeder had underestimated his foes. British intelligence had anticipated the German mission. The backbone of British strategy was the Home Fleet, based at Scapa Flow in the Orkney Islands. Admiral Sir John Tovey was ordered to intercept, covering the passages into the Atlantic on either side of Iceland with his cruisers, while his main force, two squadrons capable of dealing with the Germans, waited to engage. When Admiral Gunther Lutjens, in command of the *Bismarck*, left Bergen in Norway on 21 May the trap was already set.

Early on 23 May the cruisers HMS *Norfolk* and HMS *Suffolk* intercepted the German warships in the Denmark Strait, north of Iceland, and kept contact using their radar. The

Sinking the unsinkable: the loss of the Bismarck *marked the decisive moment in the Battle of the Atlantic*

following morning the brand new battleship HMS *Prince of Wales* and the old battlecruiser HMS *Hood* arrived. Although 20 years old and in need of a major refit, the 'mighty *Hood*' was still the biggest ship in the fleet and the most potent symbol of British power. As the two forces closed, *Hood* leading the British squadron, they opened fire at over 25,000 yards, the limits of visual range. It was Empire Day. Within minutes, astonishingly accurate German gunnery saw both ships hit the *Hood*. A 15-inch shell penetrated her after magazine and several hundred tons of high explosive ripped the 44,000-ton ship into three almost unrecognisable fragments. She sank inside three minutes, leaving only three survivors from her 1,400 crew. The Germans immediately shifted their fire onto the *Prince of Wales*, scoring a devastating hit on her bridge while her main armament was suffering teething troubles. Even so, she hit the *Bismarck* three times before breaking off the action and rejoining the shadowing cruisers. Those hits cut the German ship's speed to 28 knots, contaminated much of her fuel, and flooded part of the ship. Amidst the euphoria of victory, Admiral Lutjens knew his mission was over; he had to head for France to repair his ship. That night, in appalling weather, the aircraft carrier HMS *Victorious* flew off nine Swordfish torpedo bombers. They scored a single hit, which wrecked the damage control work of the past 12 hours. Admiral Tovey was closing fast with two more capital ships, and only needed to keep contact to resume the battle. Then, at 03.00 on the 25th, the *Bismarck* managed to break radar contact and disappeared, and *Prinz Eugen* escaped. Tovey believed the Germans had doubled back for Norway.

Back in London, the Royal Navy was facing a crisis: their most famous ship had been destroyed and the enemy had escaped. Now every significant warship in range converged on the North Atlantic. Critically, Force H, including the aircraft carrier HMS *Ark Royal*, was ordered north from Gibraltar, while the battleship HMS *Rodney* was recalled from a voyage to the United States. Churchill added a flourish to the calm professional work of the staff, signalling simply 'Sink the *Bismarck*'.

Lutjens made the next move, and it was a serious mistake. Unaware that German radar could pick up British transmissions at far longer ranges than Britain's own, which were limited to 35,000 yards, he believed he was still being tracked. Early on 25 May he sent three long signals to Berlin: British Radio Direction Finding stations intercepted them and pinpointed his direction. That evening, as the British ships hurried to regain contact, a Luftwaffe message confirmed the course. The following morning, intelligence gained from the top secret 'Ultra' decoding was confirmed by an RAF flying boat. On her current course and speed *Bismarck* would reach land-based air cover before the British warships could catch her. She had to be stopped.

The only asset left in the British locker was the *Ark Royal*, already the most famous ship in the fleet, her outstanding war record backed up by a starring role in a film and endless German propaganda claims that she had been sunk. That afternoon, having detached the cruiser HMS *Sheffield* to gain radar contact with the *Bismarck*, the *Ark* flew off a Swordfish

Some of the 110 survivors of the Bismarck *are rescued by the British cruiser HMS* Dorsetshire

strike. In their anxiety, the aircrew launched a brilliant attack on the wrong ship – the *Sheffield* itself, which only escaped injury as a result of defective torpedo detonators. A severely chastened strike force returned to base, and another 15 Swordfish flew off into the fading light. Once again they executed a near-perfect attack, this time on the right vessel, catching the *Bismarck* between two groups of torpedoes converging at an angle of 90 degrees. Two hits were scored and no aircraft were lost. One torpedo did little damage. But the second crippled the biggest battleship afloat, striking the *Bismarck*'s Achilles heel: poor design and whiplash effect caused the stern to collapse onto the ship's rudders, then hard over to port to avoid the torpedoes. With her rudders locked in position, *Bismarck* could only steam in circles. She was just 400 miles from safety. Before the Germans could react, Captain Philip Vian arrived with five destroyers. Vian ignored orders in favour of the Nelsonian maxim of steering toward the sound of the guns. Throughout the night he wore down the Germans with a series of torpedo attacks while *Sheffield* directed Tovey in for the kill.

Tovey, in HMS *King George V*, waited until after daybreak before his flagship and *Rodney* approached. Firing began at 08.45 on 27 May at around 20,000 yards. Initially *Bismarck* shot well, her salvoes bracketing the *Rodney*, but by 09.00 her rate of fire and accuracy faltered as *Rodney*'s massive 16-inch shells struck home. *Bismarck* scored no hits. The British ships then closed to 11,000 yards. Within 45 minutes they had reduced their opponent to a helpless wreck, which was sunk by torpedoes from HMS *Dorsetshire*. Only 110 men were rescued from a crew of over 2,000.

In the following days *Prinz Eugen* escaped to Brest, but the German supply ships were destroyed. Wartime mythology had transformed the *Bismarck* into an unsinkable wonder ship, but she had proved to be deeply flawed. Never again would the Germans send their heavy warships into the Atlantic; never again would Britain be so close to defeat. It was a decisive moment for the Battle of the Atlantic, and for the war. After the *Bismarck* sortie the Germans relied on U-boats to fight the battle, and they were unable to stop the flow of food, fuel, weapons and men across the Atlantic that culminated in D-Day and the defeat of the Nazi regime.

The Royal Navy demonstrated, once again, that it was master of the oceans and of the art of war at sea. The challenge of the *Bismarck* prompted a response of global proportions, an epic pursuit and a devastating combination of carrier air strikes and heavy gunnery. The confidence and self-belief of every man, from Churchill and his admirals to the airmen and sailors, was in marked contrast to the Wagnerian fatalism of the Germans. Both sides knew that the Royal Navy was the best, and despite the loss of their talisman, HMS *Hood*, the British added a fresh glory to their record, reducing the pride of Germany to a heap of tangled scrap on the floor of the Atlantic. It was one of the Royal Navy's greatest victories.

Boudicca
Ian Drury

Since Monty Python's *Life of Brian*, the question 'what have the Romans ever done for us?' has been answered by an impressive list: roads, baths, central heating, plumbing… Yet these trappings of civilisation were enjoyed by only a tiny minority of the inhabitants of the Roman province of Britannia. For the overwhelming majority the Roman occupation meant the slaughter of their ruling class and its replacement by a foreign aristocracy. While the native kingdoms had practised slavery, the Romans organised it on an industrial scale to work their land, build their villas and dig their mines. The Romans dotted their conquered territory with new towns, but only five per cent of the population lived in them; so while a handful of Latin-speakers reclined in heated rooms, sipping wine and nibbling olives, most ordinary Britons tilled the fields of their new masters. But they did not give in without a fight.

History is written by the victors, yet in the case of Boudicca and the tribes who fought the Romans in AD 60–61, it was written by the children and great-grandchildren of the victors. No native voice will ever be heard. The nearest we have to a contemporary source is the work of Publius Tacitus (*c*.55–120), a successful politician whose father-in-law governed Britannia from 78–85. Our other source is Cassius Dio; born in 164, he served as a senator, a consul and ultimately a provincial governor. Tacitus wrote famously cryptic prose, wide open to interpretation; Cassius Dio can be equally obscure and was not as discriminating in his source material.

Between the invasion in AD 43 and the revolt, the Romans imposed their control on England as far north as the River Humber. When the rebellion began, Suetonius Paulinus, the Roman governor, was in Wales with the main strength of the Roman army. His objective was the Isle of Anglesey, the last bastion of the ancient Druids.

Boudicca was the wife of Prasutagus, king of the Iceni tribe that inhabited modern-day East Anglia; they had – so they thought – made their peace with the Romans after losing a battle in AD 48. With no male heir, Prasutagus bequeathed his kingdom to his two daughters, adding Roman Emperor Nero as co-heir in an attempt to preserve his realm. But when he died, the Romans seized the estates of the Iceni chiefs and plundered their territories. To ram home the point, his daughters were raped and Boudicca flogged. Tacitus adds that the Iceni were already in league with the neighbouring Trinovantes, who had been deprived of their lands too. Perhaps a rising was being planned when Boudicca and her girls were brutalised.

The tribes vented their fury on the Roman colonists at Colchester. The Romans must have had some warning of what was coming, thanks to the torching of outlying farms and a stampede of panic-stricken Roman families. The small garrison was reinforced from London by 200 men, but the tribesmen made short work of them. Legio IX Hispana marched to the rescue, intending to put a quick stop to the rising, but was itself cut to pieces.

Both Roman writers describe Boudicca riding in her chariot around the tribal army, making a stirring speech. Cassius Dio says she was the leader who roused the tribes to rebel and commanded them in battle. Tall, tawny-haired and clearly a history buff (her speech includes references to Ancient Egypt and Assyria), she contrasts the hardiness of her tribe with the effete ways of Rome, men who bathe in warm water, sleep – with boys – on soft couches, and are content to be ruled by an incestuous pervert like Nero. Inventing such speeches was part of the classical historical tradition: the words attributed to Boudicca reveal that the Romans shared the ambivalence of later imperial nations in their attitude to 'native' peoples. Boudicca and her kin were tough, brave and unaccountably reluctant to be governed by a self-appointed European clique. Tacitus was a former legionary commander and knew what Roman conquest meant for peoples unfortunate enough to occupy real estate his masters coveted.

With a legion destroyed and Colchester a smouldering ruin, Boudicca's vengeance continued. Chelmsford suffered the same fate: excavations there reveal the same thick layer of ash dated to this time. London was next.

Paulinus rode ahead of his men to find a defenceless city in panic. The governor rode back to meet his troops, Legio XIV and Legio XX, force-marching from Wales, and ordered Legio II Augusta to join him from its base in the West Country. Dio dwells in salacious detail on the inventive tortures inflicted by Boudicca's kinsmen on the citizens of the towns they sacked, and claims that 80,000 people were massacred, though the slaughter is probably exaggerated: archaeological records prove these towns were burned, but there are few skeletal remains. Certainly London was rebuilt and repopulated very quickly for a city whose inhabitants are all supposed to have died in AD 61.

The Britons pursued Paulinus until they met him in battle, somewhere in the midlands. He was a legion short: for some reason Legio II Augusta literally sat on its laurels. (Its disgraced camp prefect later committed suicide.) Paulinus had more than 10,000 men in the field: two legions plus auxiliary infantry and cavalry. Boudicca is credited with the usual vast horde ascribed to tribal armies by Roman authors: their accounts read like a Roman version of *Zulu* ('the scouts report Britons, sir, to the south-east … thousands of them'). Paulinus deployed his army across a clearing in a narrow, wooded valley and the Britons charged. Boudicca's warriors had swords and spears, but no body armour. They carried shields, but the Romans threw javelins that tended to stick in the shield (if they did not hit the victim), forcing the owner to discard his sole form of protection. The Romans had stout shields and interlocking armour plate, their steel helmets reminiscent of modern riot-control equipment. Their impetus broken by the shower of javelins, the Britons slogged it out against the most expert swordfighters of the ancient world. Little by little they were shunted back, onto the wagons bearing their families and their loot. It became an exercise in crowd control, with knives.

Tacitus reported 400 Roman dead; given his access to source material, this is credible and indicates a hard-fought battle. Taking the rule-of-thumb estimate of two wounded to

The warrior queen: Thomas Thorneycroft's famous bronze statue of Boudicca and her daughters

each man killed, Roman casualties would have come close to ten per cent of the army, a very high proportion: in ancient history the victors usually suffered comparatively few losses, since the real killing did not begin until the soldiers of one side tried to run away. For Paulinus and his men, it was home for tea and medals. Legio XIV Gemina became Legio XIV Gemina Victrix and the hitherto untagged Legio XX became Legio XX Valeria Victrix.

For Boudicca – whose army, despite having no supply arrangements, no discipline and only the most informal command structure, had sacked four towns and travelled halfway across the country when it fought its final battle – defeat meant the extermination of her dynasty and oblivion for her people. Tacitus says she committed suicide; Dio has her falling sick and dying. The fate of her daughters is unknown. The revenge of Paulinus and his legions was terrible indeed – so savage as to arouse critical comment from Tacitus: as always with the Romans, victory was followed by the elimination of native rulers (bar a few abject collaborators) and the effective enslavement of the population. Nothing is heard again of the Iceni, or the Druids, or Boudicca, until the writings of Tacitus were rediscovered in the Renaissance.

Playwrights, novelists, sculptors and historians have subsequently come up with at least seven ways of spelling her name, and many more of spinning a complex story from a few pages of Latin text and a foot of ash under London. Successive generations cast Boudicca in whatever light suited them: Jacobean dramatists used her as a vehicle for post-Elizabethan misogyny; Lloyd George hailed her as one of the heroes of Wales when he unveiled J. Harvard Thomas' statue of her and her two voluptuous daughters in 1916. Thomas Thorneycroft's famous statue of the warrior queen next to the Houses of Parliament is perhaps the most enduring image. It is wildly inaccurate: the horses are far bigger than the ponies of ancient Britain; her chariot has solid wheels (they should be spoked) and the infamous scythe blades projecting from the hubs are pure invention. On the plus side, her flimsy robe leaves little to the imagination, and her daughters ride topless – Victorian artists needed no lessons from Hollywood in gratuitous nudity. In 2003 Ann Widdecombe argued for Boudicca's inclusion in the '100 Worst Britons' for the sack of London, presumably unaware that Boudicca shared her opposition to at least one field sport (hares were sacred to the Britons: it was the Romans who introduced hare coursing). The recent TV mini-series starring Alex Kingston as the flame-haired warrior queen made her a real-life *Xena: Warrior Princess* with a dash of Celtic magic.

In the darkest days of 1940, when this country faced invasion by the Nazis, Churchill refused to capitulate. If our island story is to end, he told his Cabinet, let it not do so until the last of us lies choking in his own blood. Boudicca and her warriors put his brave words into practice.

Winston Churchill's 1940 speeches
Andrew Roberts

'Rhetorical power,' wrote Winston Churchill, 'is neither wholly bestowed, nor wholly acquired, but cultivated.' He certainly worked hard to cultivate his own oratorical powers, spending hours in front of the mirror as a young man, testing out words, practicing phrases and honing his verbal flourishes. He disliked speaking impromptu, relied heavily on notes and written texts, and thought nothing during the Second World War of spending ten to twelve hours working on an important speech. He was a perfectionist rather than a born orator, and in 1940 the result was pure perfection.

The cadences of Churchill's 1940 speeches owe much to the hours when, as a young hussar subaltern stationed in India nearly half a century earlier, he had studied the historical works of Gibbon and Macaulay. Churchill created his own synthesis of the grandiloquent rolling sentences of the former and the biting wit of the latter. His oratory was also informed by the late-Victorian influences of William Gladstone, the Irish-American politician Bourke Cockran and his own father, Lord Randolph Churchill.

This grand, old-style idiom did not impress everybody: some found it insincere, others pompous; yet others derided him as a cross between a ham actor and a music-hall turn. There was even one point in the devil's decade of the 1930s when the House of Commons refused to listen to him and shouted him down when he tried to defend King Edward VIII during the Abdication Crisis.

It was not really until the *annus mirabilis* of 1940 that, in that supreme test of the British people, Churchill's rhetoric at last truly matched the perils of the hour to create the sublime beauty of the best of his wartime speeches. The defeat on the Western Front, the evacuation from Dunkirk, the Fall of France, the Battle of Britain, the Blitz, the threat of invasion – all produced speeches and phrases that will live as long as does the English tongue.

The printed page is not the correct medium for them, of course. To feel the shiver down one's spine at Churchill's words, only recordings will do. They alone can convey the growls, the strange pronunciation of the letter 's', the almost comic sound of 'Narzees', the sudden leonine roars, the perfectly constructed sentences, the cigar-and-brandy-toned voice, the sheer defiance coming straight from the viscera, insisting upon no surrender in a war to the death.

In the summer of 1940, Churchill's speeches were just about all the British people had to sustain them. With Hitler in control of all continental Europe from Brest to Warsaw, even the chiefs of staff had no logical plan for victory. With neither Russia nor America in the conflict, all Britain could do was hold on, grimly praying that something might turn up. Churchill could not really appeal to the head in his protestations of the certainty of ultimate victory, so he had to appeal to the heart.

Without having very much in the way of sustenance or good news for the British people, Churchill took a political risk in deliberately choosing to emphasise the dangers instead.

Three days after becoming Prime Minister, he told the House of Commons: 'I have nothing to offer but blood, toil, tears and sweat.' He attempted no evasions about the nature of the task ahead, as his words swept away a decade of appeasement, doubt and defeatism, what he had called at the time of Munich 'the long, drawling tides of drift and surrender'. He unhesitatingly placed the conflict in the stark context of a Manichean struggle between Good and Evil, Truth and Falsehood, Right and Wrong. It was what Britons longed to hear.

The effect was extraordinary. As the writer Vita Sackville-West told her husband, the Information Minister Harold Nicolson: 'One of the reasons why one is stirred by his Elizabethan phrases is that one feels the whole massive backing of power and resolve behind them, like a great fortress: they are never words for words' sake.' The mention of Elizabethan England is instructive, for Churchill enlisted the past into service to boost British morale, summoning up the ghosts of Drake and Nelson to emphasise to the people that Britain had faced such dangers before and had prevailed. He did this very deliberately in his post-Dunkirk speech in the House of Commons on 4 June, where he mentioned the threat of Napoleon. His peroration in that speech contained the famous words:

> We shall go on to the end. We shall fight in France, we shall fight on the seas and oceans, we shall fight with growing confidence and growing strength in the air, we shall defend our Island, whatever the cost may be, we shall fight on the beaches, we shall fight on the landing grounds, we shall fight in the fields and in the streets, we shall fight in the hills; we shall never surrender.

It has been pointed out by linguistics experts that every single word employed in that passage, barring one, came directly from the Old English tongue of the Anglo-Saxons. The only foreign word was 'surrender', which came from the French.

Churchill's own rhetorical finest hour came on 18 June 1940 when he made a speech in the House of Commons designed to banish the possibility, widely considered abroad, that Britain might follow France's example of the previous day and sue for peace. The peroration of this address bears extensive quotation, both for its lion-hearted resolve and for the superb English in which it was couched:

> What General Weygand called the Battle of France is over. I expect the Battle of Britain is about to begin. Upon this battle depends the survival of Christian civilisation. Upon it depends our own British way of life, and the long continuity of our institutions and our Empire. The whole fury and might of the enemy must very soon be turned on us. Hitler knows he must break us in this Island or lose the war. If we can stand up to him, all Europe may be free and the life of the world may move forward into broad, sunlit uplands. But if we fail, then the whole world, including the United States, including all that we have known and cared for, will sink into the abyss of a new Dark Age made more sinister, and perhaps more protracted, by the

'He mobilised the English language and sent it into battle': Winston Churchill in 1940

lights of perverted science. Let us therefore brace ourselves to our duties, and so bear ourselves that, if the British Empire and its Commonwealth last for a thousand years, men will still say 'This was their finest hour.'

Sir Isaiah Berlin, in his superb essay 'Mr Churchill in 1940', was at pains to point out how Churchill drew on 'an historical imagination so strong, so comprehensive as to encase the whole of the present and the whole of the future in a framework of a rich and multi-coloured past'. Churchill expected at least a working knowledge of British history from his listeners; he never talked down to them or patronised them by adapting his style to the perceived requirements of a modern mass audience. As Berlin put it: 'The archaisms of style to which Mr Churchill's wartime speeches accustomed us are indispensable ingredients of the heightened tone, the formal chronicler's attire, for which the solemnity of the occasion called.'

From the perspective of today's politics and society, much of Churchill's argument and the vocabulary in which it was couched was deeply politically incorrect. The revisionist historian Clive Ponting has complained of the way Churchill continually referred to 'our own British life, and the long continuity of our institutions and the Empire', instead of 'coming up with a view of the future designed to appeal to a modern democracy'. This was because Churchill realised that the British nation was fighting for its very identity and continued existence, rather than for any utopian ideas about decency, fraternity or democracy. He therefore appealed to a visceral, ancient, tribal belief that the British people then had in themselves, largely based on the deeds of their forefathers and pride in their imperial achievement. It is sadly no longer an idiom politicians can turn to, but it saved us then.

There are those, such as Lord Hailsham, who consider the emergence of Winston Churchill as Prime Minister in May 1940, within hours of Hitler unleashing his Blitzkrieg upon the West, as one of the proofs of the existence of God. No theologian, I prefer to subscribe to the opinion of the American broadcaster Ed Murrow on the phenomenon of Churchill in 1940: 'He mobilised the English language, and sent it into battle.'

The Battle of Crécy
Matthew Bennett

On 25 August 1346 King Edward III led a small force with its back to the wall. His 8,000 men were opposed by three times that number of angry Frenchmen, out for his and his followers' blood. For Edward had invaded France six weeks earlier and created a trail of destruction from Normandy to the Valley of the Seine, even threatening Paris. Unable to breach its formidable defences, and fearing encirclement by superior French forces, on 16 August he retreated northwards to friendly territory. This meant Ponthieu, where he held lands by right of his mother, including the port of Le Crotoy at the mouth of the River Seine. Here he had arranged to have supplies transported across the Channel for just such an eventuality as he now found himself in.

The French king, Philip VI, however, was not about to let him go unpunished for his temerity. Philip gathered an army of some 20,000 knights and men-at-arms, supported by specialist infantry – several thousand 'Genoese' crossbowmen – and set off in hot pursuit. The outcome of the ensuing battle, fought near the village of Crécy, depended in large part upon the contest between the English bowmen and the Genoese.

Calling the bowmen 'English' is a convention, because they fought in the army of the King of England. It would be more accurate to call them British, because many of them were Welsh. Edward's army also included Irish foot-soldiers, renowned for their brutality and rapacity on campaign. Only Scots were missing from the full British mix (*pace* Shakespeare's *Henry V*, performed before the Scottish King James I), because Edward was at war with their country, which was in alliance with France. Indeed, English archery led to the defeat and capture of David II, King of Scots, at Neville's Cross (near Durham) only a couple of months after Crécy.

Archers made up more than half of Edward's small force. They carried six-foot-long simple stave bows, now commonly called longbows. The tough men who wielded them, and the mighty weapon itself, can truly be called 'great'. Every one of them had trained from childhood to pull the huge weights of the 'great bow of war'. The English kings had been recruiting such archers in large numbers since the Welsh wars of the late 13th century. In Edward's reign, they had already proved their worth in battle against the Scots (Halidon Hill, outside Berwick, in 1333) and versus the French in Brittany (especially at Morlaix in 1342). King Edward could be very confident that if he chose a good defensive position and his enemy attacked him rashly, his archers would cut them down in swathes. This is exactly what he contrived on that hot summer's day in 1346. This, too, was a great piece of generalship. It is possible that he knew the lie of the land very well and that, like another great general, the Duke of Wellington, he had made an assessment of good places to fight should he need to.

Overleaf: *French crossbows meet English longbows: the Battle of Crécy as seen by a 15th-century artist*

Edward first had to get lucky, though. His retreat northwards was blocked by the River Somme, now canalised and tamed but six centuries ago a wide and swampy obstacle to his line of march, with its bridges defended by French troops. Again, local knowledge came into play as he marched, seemingly illogically, towards the mouth of the great river, two miles broad. He had discovered by intelligence that there was a ford, accessible at low-tide. It was known as Blanchetaque (White Spot) ford, because in order to get across it safely the forders had to keep their eyes on a white cliff on the northern bank. Early in the morning of 24 August the English army made its crossing. This should not have been easy, because a French force of 500 men-at-arms and 3,000 infantry had been told to prevent it. But wading knee- to waist-deep in the water, the English archers showered their missiles on the enemy on the opposing bank, forcing them to fall back. This created a bridgehead for their own mounted men-at-arms to drive off the defenders and allow the whole army to cross safely. The next night, Edward's men camped on a hillside next to Crécy, acutely aware that the main French army was hot on their heels.

Philip VI was keen for revenge; even more so were his nobles, who had felt humiliated by early reversals in the war and by what they considered too cautious a policy by their ruler. Now it seemed as if they had the English in a trap. The plan was for the crossbowmen to precede an assault. Their shooting was intended to neutralise the English archery and allow the superior French cavalry to ride down the enemy. But although the crossbow was a powerful weapon, capable of piercing any armour, it had a major drawback: it was very slow to reload. The stiff arms of the bow could only be bent by winding a ratchet device that every crossbowman wore on his belt, reducing the 'rate of fire' to little more than one a minute. During the time spent reloading the bow, its user needed to shelter behind a tall, rectangular shield known as a 'pavise'.

On the morning of 26 August, the French were rushing headlong to attack the English, fearing that they might slip away if they were not 'pinned' by an assault. As a result, the pavises, which were carried in wagons accompanying the French army, got left behind, denying the crossbowmen their essential protection in the firefight. Meanwhile, Edward had not been idle in preparing his army's defences. He had taken his stand on a hill topped by a windmill (which he used as command post). Behind this position lay a wood, and between it and the hill, where the army was deployed, Edward established his camp. This was not just a few tents, but an area filled with his men's horses and surrounded by wagons to form a barricade. This construction protected the English army from being attacked in flank or rear by the mobile French cavalry. For, remarkably, Edward had chosen to fight on foot. He dismounted his heavily armoured nobles, knights and men-at-arms in such a way as to support his lightly protected archers in the mêlée. In addition, his wild Irish foot were poised to hurl themselves under the bellies of the charging enemy, disembowelling or hamstringing their mounts. In order to reduce the impetus of the anticipated French charge, he also ordered that his archers dig 'pottes' (potholes) in front of the position. These are described as being a foot square and deep, and were intended to trip up the charging horses. Edward's deployment seems to have placed his armoured men in the centre and the archers on the flanks, to give them a clear field of fire.

As the French approached, the crossbowmen were sent out in front as planned; but their shooting was totally ineffective. One reason for this was that a summer thunderstorm had soaked the cords of their bows, reducing their strength. In contrast, the English archers had been able swiftly to remove their own bowstrings, coil them and pop them under their headgear, keeping them dry so that their own shooting was unimpaired. As a result, the crossbowmen, lacking their shields and with shortened range and impact, were massacred and driven back. The French cavalry, already distrustful of foreigners and their fancy gadgets, cried treason and charged through the scattering mob to get to hand-strokes with their hated foe. Except that many of them, too, never made it. The archers had a variety of arrows at their disposal: some with bodkin (needle) heads for piercing armour and others winged to gash and tear flesh. These were the type used for hunting, and they proved particularly effective against the French horses. Many, maddened by their wounds, bolted, threw their riders or veered off course. Those that did survive stumbled into the potholes. The French deserve credit for persevering in their attacks – as many as 15 are recounted by contemporary sources – but their assaults were fruitless. Some did break through to the men-at-arms, but here too they met stiff opposition. Edward, Prince of Wales (later known as 'The Black Prince') was fighting in the front line. Famously, King Edward declined to send reinforcements to his beleaguered son, saying that it was right for him to win his spurs unsupported. He did, as did his troops. The French apparently left 1,500 men of rank dead upon the battlefield, identifiable by the heralds from their coats of arms; English losses were negligible. Crécy was truly a great victory in an era of British military greatness.

Oliver Cromwell
Frank Kitson

Contrary to popular belief, Cromwell was not a leading player in the civil war that raged in England between 1642 and 1646. At the start he was commissioned as a captain to raise a troop; in 1643 he commanded a regiment; in 1644 he became second-in-command of the Eastern Association Army, which was one of several regional armies. On 11 June 1645, one day before the battle of Naseby, he joined Parliament's main army, known as the New Model Army, as second-in-command to Sir Thomas Fairfax, a brilliant professional soldier who had raised, trained and directed it from its inception two and a half months earlier. Cromwell was still Fairfax's second-in-command when the war ended one year later. Why then do so many people insist on crediting him with the direction of Parliament's armies during this time?

The simple answer is that they are wrong, and have probably become confused by the fact that Cromwell eventually became head of state and, in the view of many historians, the man who laid the foundations of the modern British Army. Another reason may be that they overestimate the political influence that he had in 1642 and suppose that his military position reflected it. In fact, his political influence in 1642 was minimal and it only grew as his military career developed. The most important thing Cromwell did between 1642 and 1646 was to develop an original method of raising and training his regiment. It was based on his conviction that well disciplined and godly men who, in his own words, 'know what they fight for and love what they know' would achieve more than men who joined for money or loot or because they were grabbed by the next army that passed by. Not only did he apply this system to his regiment, but he also spread it first to the Eastern Association Army and finally to the New Model Army itself. Discipline, training and motivation were the keys to his success.

Cromwell first became widely known after the battle of Marston Moor, when the Eastern Association Army joined with the Scottish and the Northern Armies to fight Prince Rupert outside York. Despite the fact that these armies greatly outnumbered the Royalists, they nearly lost the battle in the first half-hour. Indeed they might well have done so had not Cromwell, who was in charge of the left wing, managed, with his four regiments of horse, to fight the enemy opposing him to a standstill. This gave the allies a chance to recover, and they went on to win. Cromwell rightly received much credit, which was not greatly dented by his lacklustre performance at the second battle of Newbury later in the year.

At the end of 1644 a frustrated Cromwell returned to Parliament, having fallen out with his general. Parliament too was frustrated. Although the victory at Marston Moor had given it control of the north, its main army, commanded by the Earl of Essex, had been destroyed

Old Ironsides: Oliver Cromwell, the father of the British Army, around 1649

in Cornwall, and the subsequent combination of two regional armies had failed to defeat the king at Newbury. For this reason a number of prominent Parliamentarians, including Cromwell, forced through measures to replace all the existing armies with the New Model Army, backed by some local regiments and garrison troops. These arrangements brought the first civil war to an end in June 1646.

After this a rift developed between Parliament and its army over a number of issues, such as fair payment for regiments being disbanded and the future government of the country. Parliament was dominated by Presbyterians who were, so to speak, the establishment Puritans, closely allied to the Scots, whereas the army was largely under the influence of the Independents. The Independents spent much time in prayer bewailing the sins of the world, but the intensity of their religion, which bolstered their courage and reinforced their discipline, made them formidable as fighting men. In 1647 Cromwell, who was both an Independent and an MP, did what he could to bring the parties together, as a result of which he gained much political influence. Only now could it be said that he was one of the leading men in the country.

The second civil war of 1648 only lasted for a few months. It consisted of a major uprising in the south-east and a minor one in Wales, followed by an invasion by a badly organised army of Scottish Royalists in the north-west. Fairfax handled the uprising in England, sending Cromwell to sort out Wales before going on to beat the Scots. It was Cromwell's first campaign as an independent commander and it involved him in a rapid march from South Wales to Yorkshire, collecting regiments as he went. Within six days of arriving, he attacked and destroyed an army twice the size of his own in a series of engagements known to history as the battle of Preston. His success derived from the fact that he risked getting behind the main body of the Scottish army to crush various detachments of it, one by one, without ever giving them the opportunity to combine their whole force against him.

Having done so, Cromwell took his men to Edinburgh to deal with Scotland. He arrived back in London on 6 December to find that earlier in the day Colonel Pride had forcibly ejected most of the Presbyterians from Parliament. Cromwell claimed that he had no advanced knowledge of this, but that since it had happened he was glad of it. The remains of Parliament, known as the Rump, was now in a position to dispose of the king and, with the connivance of the army and the encouragement of Cromwell, Charles I was killed at the end of the following month. The Rump then set up a Council of State as its executive body, both Fairfax and Cromwell being members of it.

In March 1649 Cromwell was given the task of subduing Ireland, where an unnatural coalition of English Royalists, Irish Protestants and Catholic insurgents was threatening the small Parliamentary garrison. Parliament was determined to regain control of that country, which might otherwise serve as a jumping-off point for Royalists aiming to return the exiled Prince of Wales to England as Charles II. Cromwell spent some months preparing a force for this purpose, before embarking for Dublin in August. Although numerous, the enemy had no intention of being drawn into a pitched battle with Cromwell's formidable regiments, and the campaign consisted of evicting the enemy from fortified towns, thereby gaining control of the surrounding area. Drogheda and Wexford refused to surrender and were taken by storm, the defenders being slaughtered. Thereafter garrisons were usually allowed to march away with their colours. By May 1650, when Cromwell was recalled to England, most of the country was under his control. Although it was the settlement, made some years later when Cromwell was Lord Protector, that was so damaging to the native Irish, it was the massacre of the Drogheda garrison, consisting mainly of English Royalists and Irish Protestants, that is most bitterly remembered.

Cromwell's recall had been brought about by the fact that Charles II had been proclaimed king in Scotland, and it was assumed that another Scots invasion was contemplated. Parliament decided to preempt this by invading Scotland, but Fairfax declined to command the expedition and resigned on 26 June 1650. Only now did Cromwell become Parliament's Commander-in-Chief.

Cromwell planned his campaign carefully to ensure that his army did not run out of supplies before he could capture an all-weather port through which it could be replenished. Advancing on Leith, he was twice repulsed by the Scottish commander, David Leslie, before he succeeded in defeating him soundly at Dunbar and consolidating his hold throughout the south of Scotland. Dunbar itself was a tactical masterpiece. Cromwell wintered around Edinburgh and then in 1651 took Perth. Meanwhile the Scottish army left Stirling, accompanied by the new king, and slipped into England in an attempt to reach London before Cromwell could overhaul it. It only reached Worcester before being halted by forces collected in the south by the Council of State. Meanwhile Cromwell arrived, taking under command the various detachments from the south. His combined force was now more than twice as strong as the enemy army, which he totally destroyed in the ensuing battle. Faced for the first time as an independent commander by a competent opponent, Cromwell had proved himself an excellent strategist and tactician.

But although Cromwell's tactical, strategic and logistic arrangements were highly effective, from a military point of view his greatest achievement was the way in which he trained, disciplined and motivated his men. It is this that represents his most enduring legacy – a legacy still remembered after 360 years – and it is for this that he is regarded by many as the father of the British Army.

Surprisingly perhaps, some even credit him with fathering democracy in England, despite the fact that he used his soldiers to turn out Parliament in 1653 and thereafter to support his rule as Lord Protector. But that's another story.

The Dambusters Raid
John Sweetman

Listeners to the BBC news on Monday 17 May 1943 learnt that 'in the early hours of
this morning, a force of Lancasters of Bomber Command led by Wing Commander G. P.
Gibson DSO DFC' had successfully 'attacked with mines' the massive dams of large
German reservoirs. A legend was born.

Striking headlines – 'Floods Pour through the Ruhr', 'Bomb-wrecked Dams Paralyse
Germany's Key Industrial Areas' – prefaced press accounts of the raid. Sensational
reconnaissance photos of the intact dam walls before the operation, the large V-shaped
gaps torn in them, and the swathe of devastation wrought by the raging torrent below
accompanied the text. Sketch maps illustrated the scope of destruction; weekly and monthly
magazines, journals and newsreels elaborated the tale.

Throughout the world, Operation Chastise – what the Secretary of State for Air Sir
Archibald Sinclair termed 'an epic feat of arms' – attracted attention and comment. Of
the 147 airmen involved, many came from the Commonwealth; one was an American.
Addressing the joint houses of Congress in Washington, Winston Churchill highlighted
the operation to resounding applause.

Twelve years later, the film *The Dam Busters*, backed by its stirring theme music, enhanced
the legend. To cinema audiences then and ever since, swelled by viewers of the regular repeats
on television, this remains the authentic account, revolving around the dogged persistence of
a civilian engineer and a photogenic squadron commander. However, in 1955 Air Chief
Marshal Sir Arthur Harris' wartime deputy, Air Marshal Sir Robert Saundby, protested that
the feasibility of attacking German dams had been studied long before Barnes Wallis became
involved. Moreover, the celluloid image of Wallis valiantly overcoming obstructive
bureaucrats and hostile senior officers was highly misleading. Once official documents were
declassified, Saundby's stance would be vindicated and the film's historical limitations
exposed, though without diminishing the pivotal roles of Wallis or Gibson.

Operation Chastise had had a protracted gestation period. In 1937 the Air Ministry
and Bomber Command began examining ways of destroying important dams to neutralise
industrial production by releasing the contents of reservoirs used for the production of
hydro-electricity and, among other things, steel. The following year Air Intelligence
concluded that 'the low-lying Ruhr valley would be flooded, so that railways, important
bridges, pumping stations and industrial chemical plants would be destroyed or rendered
inoperative'. The precise dimensions and characteristics of the proposed targets and
available means to destroy them were investigated by a wide range of individuals,
committees and departments. A succession of schemes was advanced and discarded: high-
explosive bombs dropped conventionally; torpedoes launched into the reservoirs; rockets
fired at the air side of a dam; a seaplane loaded with explosive floated downstream; even

parachutists carrying charges with which to sabotage the structure.

What emerged from these failed projects was the belief that a masonry dam like the Moehne could not be broken by a charge detonated lower than 42 feet from its crest and that any explosive must be placed in direct contact with the wall. Two crucial suggestions from the bevy of discarded schemes lingered: low-level launching of a self-propelled weapon to skim over the water; and a squadron specially trained to deliver it.

Quite independently of this process, Wallis had been seeking a means of striking at the sources of enemy industrial might, including reservoirs and dams. In 1940 he devised a 10-ton weapon to be carried in a new six-engine 'Victory' bomber and dropped from 40,000 feet. Sceptical of their viability, the Air Ministry rejected both the bomb and the bomber.

However, Wallis now had access to information already amassed by the different agencies. In 1942 he invented a projectile with enough explosive to destroy the Moehne and any similar dam. Released at low level, it would ricochet over the water, sink beside the dam and be detonated at a decisive predetermined depth in contact with it. This 'bouncing bomb', which would be back-spun, represented Wallis' unique solution to a long-standing problem.

Harris famously dismissed the idea as 'tripe of the wildest description'. The decisive voice, though, was that of Air Chief Marshal Sir Charles Portal, who had held Harris' post in 1940 when the Moehne Dam was attracting close attention. Towards the end of February 1943 he authorised the operation based on Wallis' proposal.

As yet no full-size drawing of the weapon existed. Experiments on models and a disused dam in Wales, as well as dropping trials from a Wellington at Chesil Beach in Dorset, had been carried out with scaled-down versions. Furthermore, a new squadron had to be formed and trained for the attack to take place before 26 May, later advanced to 19 May – a date determined by the water level in the reservoirs and necessary moonlight conditions.

While Guy Gibson took command of 617 Squadron at RAF Scampton in Lincolnshire, Wallis worked away in his office at Burhill Golf Club in Surrey, and test pilots dropped different sizes and shapes of his creation off Reculver in the Thames estuary.

Ultimately, the Lancaster crews would need to drop a 9,250 lb metal cylinder, spinning backwards at 500 revolutions per minute, 425–475 feet from a dam wall while travelling at 220 mph ground speed and precisely 60 feet above the water. In darkness, they must fly at 100 feet to and from the target area to minimise the impact of flak and deter prowling fighters. Contrary to the popular myth, not all aircrew were highly decorated veterans: some had flown only a handful of operations, and six of the pilots were undecorated.

On the night, six dams (four connected with the Ruhr, two with the Eder valley) were scheduled for attack. Of the 19 aircraft which took off from Scampton in three waves, three turned back before their target and eight of the remaining 16 were lost. Four dams were attacked, two of them ruptured and another damaged.

As the full story of the operation unfolded over the years, universal acclaim gave way to often savage condemnation. Critics ranged from a colour-supplement journalist asserting

Overleaf: *'An epic feat of arms': Lancasters bomb the Moehne Dam, as painted by Frank Wootten*

that 'the truth about the Dams Raid is that it was a conjuring trick, virtually devoid of military significance' to a Cambridge scientist arguing that 'the dams raid … had scant effect on German war production; the influence of the ricochet bomb on the imponderable sum of war was negligible'. TV programmes screened for the 50th anniversary added spice to these caustic allegations.

Irrefutably, the Sorpe Dam, although damaged, was not destroyed, and the breaches in the Moehne and Eder dams were repaired by October. Post-operational claims of damage, too, were patently exaggerated, and without doubt many of the figures published in the press in 1943 were wildly inaccurate. But these were based on imaginative reports from neutral countries like Switzerland and Sweden, not official communiqués. Before the operation the Air Ministry had toned down the extreme claims of pre-war optimists. Dreams of catastrophic damage to the Ruhr valley, for example, were reduced to 'appreciable … less far-reaching than had been previously been estimated'. And Wallis' influential paper, *Air Attack on Dams*, was peppered with qualifications like 'might' and 'it is possible'. Afterwards Harris referred to the raid as 'a major victory in the Battle of the Ruhr', not a terminal blow to industrial production.

Nevertheless, the physical impact of the operation was more than its critics allow. In 1949 Otto Kirschmer, a professor of engineering, explained that, in spite of Nazi denials, the Ruhr area had been 'very seriously affected' and damage below the Eder considerably underestimated. Referring to the threat of Allied bombers to military supplies in autumn 1944, the Minister for Armament and War Production, Albert Speer, observed: 'There had certainly been critical situations before this – the bombing of the Ruhr reservoirs, for instance.' The fighter commander Adolf Galland believed the raid had a 'lasting effect' on German morale. Speer confirmed that Hitler was both shaken and enraged by it.

Speer also conceded that to repair the damage 27,000 specialists and labourers were temporarily drafted from urgent work elsewhere. More permanently, anti-aircraft guns, searchlights, balloons and smoke apparatus, together with, in manpower terms, the equivalent of a whole military division, were moved from other potential targets to protect ten major dams. The water level in vulnerable reservoirs was lowered, with a consequent reduction in available water; gas and electricity supplies were never fully restored to some localities.

One of his interrogators told Flight Sergeant John Fraser, who baled out of a stricken Lancaster over the Moehne Dam, that this raid was a hundred times more effective than any hitherto. It was also timely for the inhabitants of the United Kingdom, after three years without visible success on the European mainland. In the words of an intelligence officer, Flight Lieutenant G. E. Pine, 'we did need it'.

At the time, Operation Chastise undoubtedly had vast national and international impact. A small force penetrating deep into enemy-held territory had attacked targets in Germany's industrial heartland with an extraordinary weapon delivered in accordance with specific, tight requirements. Hans Rump, a contemporary high-ranking German official, described the result as 'precision bombing of a high order'. For that alone the Dambusters Raid deserves the verdict 'an epic feat of arms'.

The Dreadnought
Andrew Lambert

In 1906 the Royal Navy changed the standard of naval power. After 15 years of stability the rulebook of battleship design was torn up. HMS *Dreadnought* was so awe-inspiring that her name became the generic term to describe all the battleships that followed. At a stroke every other battleship in the world became obsolescent, a status reinforced by the term 'pre-Dreadnought'. Now all the world's navies would have to start again.

Dreadnought was a quantum leap in all-round performance. Her turbine engines, the first to be used in a ship of this size, gave far more power than the standard reciprocating machinery, were more economical at high speed, and required only a fraction of the maintenance. These engines allowed her to reach a speed of 21 knots, at least three knots faster than her predecessors. *Dreadnought* could choose whether to fight, and at what range. The new engines were as remarkable in their way as the decision to replace piston engines on aircraft with jets. The other obvious feature was the shift from four heavy 12-inch guns to ten. With improved fire control and range-finding equipment these guns could be used together, making the new ship at least twice as powerful, and capable of effective long-range fire. It was a response to the rapid increase in the range of the torpedo, which rendered the old battle tactics of fighting at one to two miles' distance impossible. The additional heavy guns replaced the medium-calibre battery of 6-inch guns that had been so important for close-range fighting. *Dreadnought* would fight at ranges where such guns were irrelevant. Just to ram home the point, she looked completely different from her solid, staid predecessors. Her stripped-down style stressed guns and speed. Although hardly any bigger than her predecessors, *Dreadnought* embodied power: she became the defining symbol of British strength in the Edwardian age, an instant design icon.

The new ship was masterminded by one man, Admiral Sir John Fisher, First Sea Lord from 1904 to 1910. Fisher took office on Trafalgar Day 1904, and immediately assembled the best and brightest technical minds in the Royal Navy and British industry to develop his new ship. He had been thinking long and hard about the future of war at sea: *Dreadnought* was the product of one man's genius, and the advanced ideas of many more.

Yet *Dreadnought* was more than just another fighting ship. She was designed to meet other agendas. The cost of the Navy had been rising steadily since the 1890s; Britain was struggling to match the spending of her rivals. Fisher had been appointed to reduce the costs, without sacrificing strength. His improved battleship was a key part of the answer: it would be built with extreme efficiency, and other ship types would be cut out. By raising the stakes he would force other navies to stop and think about their own programmes. It was hoped that the cost would deter any serious competition.

Overleaf: *Changing the standard of naval power: HMS* Dreadnought *rules the waves*

For maximum political impact, and to test the new systems that were included in the design, the ship was built in record time. Normally battleships took between two and three years to complete. By careful planning, and a lot of prior preparation, *Dreadnought* was officially built in 12 months. Laid down at Portsmouth Dockyard in October 1905, she was at sea on 2 October 1906. For speed of development, she even 'borrowed' guns ordered for HMS *Lord Nelson*.

The debut of the *Dreadnought* was a stunning success. She gave the Royal Navy a massive lead in key new technologies, while her design was so successful that it was used for another six ships. The impact on the competition was universal. Every other navy stopped building battleships, and while they were working out what to do, Britain built ten more Dreadnoughts. Most countries simply gave up: only Germany and the United States built Dreadnought fleets before 1914. Germany was the only threat to Britain, and her challenge was derailed by the Dreadnought. Not only did it force a massive increase in the cost of her new ships, but it rendered useless the key strategic waterway, the Kiel Canal, that allowed the German fleet to move between the Baltic and the North Sea without passing round Denmark. It would take Germany eight years to widen and deepen the canal so that her own Dreadnoughts could use it; until then Germany dared not go to war with Britain. The canal was ready for service in June 1914, and war broke out in August. In the interval Britain's naval demonstrations blocked German attempts to dominate Europe. Indeed, so skilfully did Fisher play on German fears that many were convinced the Royal Navy was ready to attack without warning. By winning the naval arms race with Germany, Fisher and his Dreadnoughts served their purpose. They cut costs, increased efficiency and secured the Empire.

By 1914 the latest battleships were 'Super-Dreadnoughts', twice as big and twice as powerful as the original *Dreadnought*. She served through World War I, though ironically the only time she sank an enemy ship, when she was patrolling with the fleet on 18 March 1915, she did not use her powerful guns, but rammed and cut in half the German submarine U29; no other battleship ever sank a submarine. In 1920 *Dreadnought*, by now quite overtaken by a new icon, the 44,000-ton battlecruiser HMS *Hood*, was quietly paid off and sold for scrap.

It took another charismatic leader, Admiral Lord Louis Mountbatten, to revive the name for another epoch-making warship: Britain's first nuclear submarine of 1960 was also named HMS *Dreadnought*. She too has gone the way of all old ships, but the name will live on, and a new Dreadnought will take her place. When she does, she will be the twelfth in a line that stretches back to the heyday of Elizabethan naval power, when the first *Dreadnought* of 1573 went to sea. The Elizabethan love of compound names brought together two powerful old English words to form an inspired, poetic embodiment of the purpose of the ship. Along with those other contemporary compounds *Vanguard*, *Warspite* and *Swiftsure*, *Dreadnought* entered the naval lexicon and has remained in use for more than 400 years. In the process it has surpassed them all to become a noun, forever linked with the name of John Fisher. (In late 1909 when Fisher was made a Lord, he took as his motto the phrase 'Fear God and Dread Nought', a combination of faith, continuity and commitment that ensured the exercise of power was not spoiled by arrogance.)

Like her most famous successor, that first Elizabethan *Dreadnought* had been designed to be faster and more powerful than any rival ship. She fought with Drake when he singed the King of Spain's beard at Cadiz in 1587, helped defeat the Armada in 1588, and went back to Cadiz with Raleigh in 1596. Her successor was in the thick of the fighting against the Dutch in the 17th century, while two 18th-century *Dreadnoughts* hammered the French and the Spanish, first singly and then jointly. On the immortal 21 October 1805 it was the *Dreadnought*, coming into action near the end of the battle off Cape Trafalgar, that helped to complete the work so nobly begun by Nelson and Collingwood, her well-trained gun crews pouring in a series of shattering broadsides that ended the last flickering resistance of the French and Spanish. That celebrated ship spent many years in retirement moored off Greenwich as a hospital for seamen, and her name lives on in the old Hospital building, now a university library, alongside the Naval College.

In the 1870s there was a new *Dreadnought*, the most powerful ironclad afloat, with four massive guns and armour plate more than a foot thick, the embodiment of Victorian might. Her low freeboard, squat turrets, massive yellow funnels and black and white paintwork made her the symbol of Empire, an iron fist that deterred any rival from interfering with Britannia's command of the oceans. And when her day was done, and a new challenge arose from Germany, it was her famous name, loaded with power and glory, that was chosen to adorn the ultimate expression of modernity.

The genius of Admiral Fisher, supported by engineers and officers of the first rank, created a ship that stunned the world and gave her name – a name created more than 300 years before to defend the country from an earlier menace and revived many times over the centuries – to the future of war at sea. Linking Elizabeth and Drake, Nelson and Fisher, it symbolises the continuity and purpose that has made the Royal Navy the senior service, the bedrock of British security whereon, in the words of the Articles of War, 'under the good Providence of God, the wealth, safety, and Strength of this Kingdom chiefly depend'.

The evacuation of Dunkirk
Robin Neillands

The jury is still out on the Dunkirk evacuation, the rescue of the British Expeditionary Force from France in the summer of 1940. There are those who say it was a disaster, or at best a national humiliation. There are others who say it was a triumph of improvisation and organisation by the Royal Navy that snatched a victory from the jaws of defeat and saved Britain's army to fight another day. Few people would dispute that the end result of Operation Dynamo was a miracle.

To trace the origins of the Dunkirk evacuation it is necessary to go back to the start of the war. Britain went to war with Nazi Germany on 3 September 1939, following the German attack on Poland. Poland was rapidly defeated, but, apart from air operations and a few patrol skirmishes, nothing happened in France and Belgium – the Western Front – until the spring of 1940. This was the period of the 'Phoney War' – the *Sitzkrieg* – when everyone waited to see what Hitler would do next, and the French, with their British allies, waited behind the illusory protection of the Maginot Line, did a little training and sang hopeful songs about hanging out their washing on the Siegfried Line.

On 10 May 1940 all that changed. That day German paratroopers descended on the Belgian forts at Eben Emael, and German tanks and motorised infantry burst through the woods and hills of the Ardennes to advance north and east to join those forces already storming through Holland. This was the Western Allies' introduction to a new kind of war – *Blitzkrieg* or lightning war – a crushing combination of fast-moving tanks and tactical aircraft that swept round or over the Allied defences and soon had the defending forces in full retreat.

The Dutch were out of the war by 16 May, and the Germans then turned their full fury on the Belgians, splitting the Allied forces at Armentières, driving the French south and hustling the British Expeditionary Force (BEF) back towards Calais. By 20 May the bulk of the BEF was being driven into a gradually closing pocket around the port and beaches of Dunkirk on the Channel coast, and on 28 May, without warning, the Belgian forces surrendered, leaving their allies, French and British, fully exposed on their northern flank.

By 20 May it had already become clear to the BEF commander, General Lord Gort, that the war in France was lost and that unless the BEF was evacuated quickly it would share in the inevitable defeat and surrender of the French army. Preparations to evacuate the BEF began on 22 May with the drawing up of plans for Operation Dynamo – an evacuation of the army by the Royal Navy, commanded from Dover by Vice-Admiral Bertram Ramsay.

Ramsay was in no doubt about the scale of his task. The German Luftwaffe dominated the skies over France and the Channel, strafing and bombing the troops now making for the Dunkirk perimeter, since the RAF, having already lost many aircraft in the Battle of France, were wisely attempting to conserve men and planes for the forthcoming Battle of Britain. No prior plans had been made to evacuate the BEF before the *Blitzkrieg* – the need had never even been contemplated – and no arrangements existed to coordinate the evacuation of large numbers of troops with the enemy hard on their heels.

Ramsay began by calling for as many vessels of destroyer size as the Navy could spare and for every coastal vessel of up to 1,000 tons that his requisitioning officers could find. Ramsay was particularly eager to find passenger ferries or pleasure steamers, anything that could carry large numbers of passengers. The first plan was to lift 45,000 troops in two days. This was then extended to 120,000 troops over five days, but the timescale and the numbers continued to expand.

On 27 May a request went out to civilian yachtsmen and the owners of river craft, asking them to provide shallow draught vessels of between 30 and 100 feet in length to lift the troops off the beaches. So began the epic, the legend – and the myth – of the 'little ships of Dunkirk', a fleet of small vessels manned by civilian men and boys that sailed across the Channel to rescue the BEF from the Dunkirk beaches under bombs and shellfire.

As with many myths, there is a certain amount of truth in this story. Hundreds of craft, large and small – lifeboats, fishing smacks, drifters, Thames river cruisers, pleasure yachts – did indeed brave the narrow seas and lift soldiers from the beaches (one of them, an 18-foot wooden open boat called the *Tamzine*, is now on display at the Imperial War Museum in London), and J. B. Priestley was right when he spoke of the time 'the little ships made a journey to hell, and came back glorious'.

The tale of the little ships remains something of a myth, however, because the Royal Navy evacuated the bulk of the troops from Dunkirk. Later figures confirmed that 396 naval vessels – destroyers and sloops – lifted 206,725 men from the harbour mole and piers of Dunkirk, and 306 assorted craft took 96,139 men from the beaches, a ratio of 2:1. And yet the myth was important at the time, as we shall see, and should not be lightly dismissed.

So the evacuation began and the numbers rescued gradually rose, in spite of the Luftwaffe. By 27 May over 100,000 men had been recovered. On 28 May 16,000 soldiers, half French, half British, were lifted from Dunkirk and the beaches, although nine destroyers and many other craft were sunk or damaged by enemy action that day. On 29 May, another day of heavy air attacks, a further 14,000 came off, and the next day no fewer than 30,000 were delivered to the south coast ports, to be greeted by the ladies of the WVS with tea and buns, sandwiches – and not a few tears.

On 31 May 78,000 men were lifted in an operation that was now going on round the clock – and so it continued until the end of Dynamo on 4 June, by which time a total of 338,000 troops, 198,000 British and 140,000 French, had been taken back to Britain in some 700 assorted vessels and small craft.

During the evacuation the perimeter was held by French and British troops, and their ability to keep the Germans back was decreasing by the hour: by 26 May the area held by the Anglo-French forces had shrunk to a few square miles, and the beaches and streets of

---

Overleaf: *Survivors of the steamer* Mona's Queen, *which lifted more than 3,000 troops from the beaches of northern France before being hit by a mine*

Dunkirk were under shellfire. The German forces investing Dunkirk came from General Heinz Guderian's 19th Panzer Corps and General G. H. Reinhardt's 41st Panzer Corps. Neither general was in any doubt that, despite the stubborn resistance they were now encountering, they could quickly push through to the beaches and compel surrender. This view was probably correct, but on 29 May Adolf Hitler ordered them to leave the destruction of the British at Dunkirk to the Luftwaffe and some infantry and to resume their pursuit of the French armies to the Seine and beyond.

Various reasons have been advanced for this decision. One is that Hitler was prepared to let the British escape, provided their equipment remained behind, calculating that this would force them to accept a negotiated peace on German terms. Another theory – a more plausible one – is that Hitler recalled how the French armies had recovered from defeat in 1914 and counterattacked successfully on the Marne; the Führer had no intention of letting them regroup this time. Finally, he may have accepted Goering's claim that the Luftwaffe could stop the Dunkirk evacuation and the BEF would be forced to capitulate anyway. Whatever the true reason, the German hesitation provided a loophole through which the last of the BEF slipped away – and due credit must be paid to the 40,000 French troops who held the perimeter without hope of relief until the last ship sailed. The BEF was obliged to leave most of its heavy kit behind: 2,500 guns of various calibre, 90,000 rifles, 77,000 tons of ammunition, 84,000 trucks, hundreds of tanks and tons of petrol were destroyed or abandoned to the enemy.

The campaign in France since 10 May had cost the British some 60,000 troops, killed, wounded or missing. Even so, it is fair to say that the rescue of the BEF produced euphoria among the public in Britain, so much so that Winston Churchill felt obliged to get up in the House of Commons and advise Parliament and people that 'We must be careful not to assign to this deliverance the attributes of victory. Wars are not won by evacuations.'

Very true. So what is a fair judgment on the Dunkirk evacuation? Churchill called it a 'deliverance', and that it certainly was. But was it a victory or a defeat? Viewing the events of that violent summer from the perspective of six decades, perhaps one can safely conclude that the nine days of Dunkirk represent a defeat for the British Army, a victory for the Royal Navy, and a blessing for the British people. The epic of Dunkirk bound the nation together. Those who did not sail to Dunkirk with the Royal Navy or with the 'little ships' still felt themselves part of that great endeavour, and were thereafter united in a common resolve. From then on, led by Winston Churchill, the British people would defend their island, whatever the cost might be – and they would never surrender. Hard though it would be, the road to victory began on the beaches of Dunkirk.

The decoding of Enigma
Hugh Sebag-Montefiore

If the Battle of Waterloo was won on the playing fields of Eton, then the battle for the Enigma code during World War II was won in the common rooms at Cambridge. Many of the codebreakers who helped break the code, and particularly the all-important naval Enigma, were still students or fellows at Cambridge University when war was declared.

The code they were asked to decipher had been produced on the Enigma cipher machine which was being used by Nazi Germany's armed forces. The Enigma machine looked like a typewriter, but it had scrambling elements inside, and different enciphering procedures were adopted for different sections of Germany's armed forces. The Enigma code used by the German navy was the most difficult to break, but it was also the most important strategically. There is general agreement amongst historians that when the Bletchley Park team broke it they shortened the war by one to two years.

Most of the codebreakers were selected after their names were submitted by tutors or colleagues who were asked to put forward their brightest young men and women. Once a name was submitted, there was nothing other than an informal interview to stop the person being hired to work in one of the codebreaking huts at Bletchley Park. Security checks were only a minor barrier to entry. For example, one young woman, 18-year-old Mavis Lever, befriended a couple of German spies before she was interviewed. Yet even after they were caught, she was not only allowed to work at Bletchley Park, but was asked to work on the Enigma cipher used by the German intelligence service, the Abwehr, for transmitting its spies' reports. Fortunately, she turned out to be the perfect recruit and went on to break the Abwehr's Enigma code without anyone outside Bletchley Park being any the wiser. Alan Turing, a young don attached to King's College, Cambridge, before the war, did more than anyone else to break the naval Enigma code. Yet he was a practising homosexual at a time when such inclinations were mostly kept in the closet, a state of affairs which made him easily blackmailable. He also managed to keep the British Enigma secret, both during and after the war.

Mavis Lever was a linguist. However, the majority of those picked out were mathematicians with first class degrees. The way one of them was approached was typical. David Rees (later an eminent professor of mathematics) was visited in his rooms at Sidney Sussex College, Cambridge, during 1939 by Gordon Welchman, one of his mathematics tutors, and another Cambridge don. They told him they had a job for him connected with the war, but they would not tell him what it was or where he was to work. Eventually, the bemused Rees blurted out: 'How will I know where to report to if you won't tell me where to go?' Only then did Welchman and his companion tell him to make his way to Bletchley railway station, where he would be met and briefed. He was duly picked up at Bletchley and informed there and then that he was to work on the German Enigma.

Thanks to this informal selection procedure, Bletchley Park was full of brilliant mavericks far removed from the strait-laced bureaucrats one expects to find in the civil service. Alan Ross (later a professor of linguistics and the inventor of the concept of non-U speech made famous by Nancy Mitford's *Noblesse Oblige*) was notorious within Bletchley Park for sedating his son with laudanum and laying him out on the luggage-rack whenever they were travelling together on the train. Bentley Bridgewater, the future Secretary of the British Museum, became a legend after he chased Angus Wilson, his homosexual lover, into the lake in front of the Bletchley Park mansion after a quarrel. Angus Wilson, who was to become a well-known novelist in later life, himself suffered from uncontrollable tantrums. One was so severe that it only subsided after he had kicked in his landlady's front door. Such behaviour overshadowed even Turing's eccentricities: he chained his coffee mug to the radiator and bicycled around the countryside wearing a gas mask in order to ward off the pollen.

The codebreakers had an indomitable spirit, which they shared with most of the British population during the dark days of 1940. This was sometimes the result of having triumphed over adversity: for example Harry Hinsley, a grammar school boy who won a scholarship to study at St John's College, Cambridge, was the son of an impoverished out-of-work labourer. He played an important role in breaking the naval Enigma. Other codebreakers acquired their stiff upper lips thanks to surviving the rigours of the British public school system. As a result, difficulties encountered at Bletchley Park – the codebreakers dealing with the Enigma were not given enough equipment or personnel – led not to resigned apathy but to rebellion. Four of the codebreakers wrote a letter of complaint about their lack of resources to Churchill, who immediately instructed that they be given what they needed.

Having so many independent-minded workers could make Bletchley hard to run. In one classic exchange with Alistair Denniston, the acting head of Bletchley Park, Dilly Knox, the classics scholar and star codebreaker, stated that he was used to seeing his work through from start to finish, 'from the raw material to the final text'. He did not take kindly to its being presented to the intelligence huts by someone else, and accused Denniston of having the mentality of a grocer for expecting him to agree to the arrangement. Denniston would not back down, and wrote back: 'If you do design a Rolls Royce that is no reason why you should yourself drive the thing up to the house of a possible buyer.' However, on other occasions Denniston supported the absent-minded professor codebreakers against the Bletchley Park managers, reining in his robust deputy, Edward Travis, with the words, 'One does not expect to find the rigid discipline of a battleship among the collection of somewhat unusual civilians who form GC & CS [as Bletchley Park was known]. To endeavour to impose it would be a mistake and would not assist our war effort.'

Paradoxically, this group of non-team players created one of the most effective and creative teams ever put together – so effective, indeed, that it should be presented as a model case study to all managers, whether of scientists, business executives or football players, who instinctively shy away from individualist 'troublemakers' in the mistaken belief that only by encouraging conformity will they achieve their finest hour.

The Enigma coding machine in action on board a German train, 1940

The Battle of Goose Green
Robert Fox

Set on its bleak isthmus on the south-west of the largest of the Falkland Islands, the settlement of Goose Green endures the caprices of the South Atlantic weather the year round. This lonely stretch of grassland, with its cluster of low houses and shearing sheds, could hardly be described as strategic ground. But for two days at the end of May 1982 it became a battlefield when a battalion of British paratroopers overcame an Argentine garrison force nearly three times its size.

It was a battle out of its time for 1982, fought for nearly 20 hours almost entirely on foot. It was a day of chaos and confusion, miscalculations, mistakes – and heroism. Altogether 18 British soldiers, including five officers, of the 2nd Battalion the Parachute Regiment battle groups, were killed and 35 wounded, as were some 200 Argentines (the exact number is still uncertain). It was the first land victory of the Anglo-Argentine Falklands Conflict of 1982. It may not have won the war, but it was a turning point: the commander of the British forces, the charismatic and unpredictable Lieutenant Colonel H. Jones, and his men knew that they could have lost this quixotic war in that single afternoon of 28 May 1982, and the Falklands to British rule forever.

At first the plan was merely to raid Goose Green for a quick victory and to prevent the Argentines deploying a helicopter force from the farms there to attack British forces as they marched on their main goal, the capital Stanley to the east. But by the time Colonel Jones ordered his men to march south to prepare to attack the settlement he had bigger ideas on his mind. The British forces had been stuck round the place of their first landing on the Falklands for nearly a week and, after several disastrous losses of warships and freighters at sea, Mrs Thatcher's government in London was in need of some good news. 'If I am ordered to attack, I am not just going to raid and come out,' I recall Jones telling me. 'I will go in to take the place, and then go on to Port Stanley.' Jones and his headquarters had received a severe jolt when they heard the BBC World Service actually broadcast that his Para battalion was about to attack – an administrative slip by London which robbed him of all surprise. The Argentines knew he was coming.

The afternoon before the battle the men of 2 Para were dispersed to lie up in the tussock grass round Camilla Creek House, the only landmark for miles and within easy range of the Argentine artillery spotters with its bright red toytown roof and white walls. Harrier planes attacked down the isthmus in two strikes, like shadowy bolts dipping and weaving a few feet above the grasslands. The same afternoon two Argentines were captured, out on a forlorn patrol to find where the British were. The information they

Yomping towards victory: a British paratrooper before the attack on Goose Green

gave was muddled, but it was clear that there were more Argentines than at first thought – roughly, it seemed, the same number as the British Para force.

Just before dusk Colonel Jones gave his orders for battle the following day. It was to be a six-phase night and day attack to take Darwin Hill and seize the Goose Green settlements, with only the last two phases, the attack on the farm itself, to be completed in daylight. During the night three 105mm light guns from 29 Regiment were flown in by helicopter to Camilla Creek. As the men streamed down to the creek in the dark, the artillery began firing, shells cutting the air with the sound of tearing cardboard. At two o'clock in the morning, 'H' hour, the two forward companies A and B crossed the start line, incongruously marked by white tape like a race at a children's sports day. Across the creek two mortar teams could be clearly heard shouting coordinates as they ranged their weapons.

The two leading companies were quickly into the battle, followed half an hour later by D Company, with A company on the left flank. The Argentine artillery, four 105mm pack howitzers corralled in the Goose Green sheep pens, began firing on the Paras' main headquarters five miles away. Tracer lit the night sky, and occasionally the guns fired phosphorus rounds. The mortars joined, dozens of rounds lighting the sky with a yellow dome, and as each illumination was fired the British troops froze where they stood. From the nearby waters of Brenton Loch the frigate HMS *Arrow* fired her main 4.5-inch gun until the turret jammed and the ship had to withdraw for fear daybreak would bring the attentions of the Argentine air force.

For a brief moment everything appeared to be going according to plan. A and B Company were moving fast and nearing their first objectives at Darwin Hill and a line of gorse along the ridge running across the isthmus. Dawn came on with sporadic heavy cloud and swirling sea mist. Groups of bedraggled prisoners began gathering round the main headquarters.

In the damp light of day the British Paras found themselves in a dramatic situation. A Company was in low ground before Darwin Hill and the gorse line, where the Argentines occupied well-fortified trenches. The British mortars could provide little cover, and ran out of smoke rounds. A company became pinned, ammunition was running out, and one of the three rifle platoons had made a wasted detour trying to cross by a causeway to the south which had already been destroyed. On the right, B Company under the swashbuckling Major John Crosland had already pushed forward to the gentle slope leading to the little airfield and the home paddocks round the farm at Goose Green. H. Jones decided to move across to A Company headquarters to help remount the attack. He became focused on the problems of the company, believing this would lead to victory. He left the other units temporarily to manage on their own.

As firing continued from the Argentine trenches, Jones decided to mount his own attack, and launched a charge up a narrow gulley through the gorse. His bodyguard yelled 'Watch your back', as a position to his rear opened fire. Jones stumbled, and as he did so he was cut down by a single round from the front. Within half an hour he was dead.

Some 500 metres back, at battalion HQ, Major Chris Keeble, the second-in-command, received the terse message 'Sunray is down', meaning the colonel was dead and he was now in charge. Saying a quick prayer, he moved up to the forward headquarters on the gorse line, and soon his battalion was moving forward. The Argentines had their moment when Jones was killed, and they failed to seize it by counterattacking. As they stayed in their trenches, Corporal Dave Abols fired a 66mm anti-tank rocket and hit the target. Minutes later the Argentines on the gorse line surrendered, and the initiative passed to Keeble and his men.

In the early afternoon Keeble brought up machine guns and Milan anti-tank missiles. D Company sneaked along the beach under the sill of the land to pass along the left flank of B Company. By Darwin Hill, C Company under Major Roger Jenner passed through A Company to advance with D Company on the schoolhouse and the airfield. Down in the settlement, the islanders, who had been confined to the community hall by the Argentines, could see the paratroopers coming through the hedge of the gorse line and beginning their advance to the houses. 'There seemed so few of them, and we didn't think they would make it,' recalls Janet Hardcastle, who had a clear view from one of the windows.

The British battalion had been pulled together by the grit and determination of its NCOs and soldiers, working together instinctively as a team. Amongst them as a reporter, I was given the firm impression that anything other than achieving the objective was not on the agenda. Setbacks continued during the day, but shortly before sunset, a glowing red reminder that it was still the austral autumn, Royal Navy Harriers attacked the Argentine forces back in the settlement itself. The two strikes silenced the ground-firing 30mm and 20mm anti-aircraft guns which had raked the approaches to the airfield and stockyards. Argentine reinforcements from Stanley and Mount Kent began arriving, but took no further part militarily.

The following morning Major Keeble had arranged to discuss surrender terms with the Argentine garrison commanders. His battalion had been reinforced by an extra company of Royal Marines, and more artillery and Harrier fighters were available if things turned nasty. In a tin hut by the grass airstrip Colonel Piaggi and Air Commodore Pedrozo agreed to surrender with honour. Some 400 men in the uniforms of the marines, special forces, navy and air force paraded, sang their national hymn and laid down their weapons. Waiting by the airfield, my reporter colleague David Norris and I were astonished to see hundreds more in Argentine army uniforms come out to parade in the same fashion. Somewhere around 1,200 surrendered at the airstrip – which meant that 2 Para had been fighting at odds of three to one against, as against the norm for an assaulting force, which should try to have odds of three to one in its favour.

It was an extraordinary and eccentric victory, a drama in high colours. For some critics it was a strategically unnecessary and deliberately political battle. But it was won by the instinctive teamwork and determination of the soldiers and their NCOs – for whom retreat was never an option. It was, in the words of Major John Crosland, OC B Company, 'the ultimate come as you are party'.

The Gurkhas
Gordon Corrigan

The Gurkhas and the British have fought side by side for nearly 200 years, but they first met as enemies. In the latter half of the 18th century the Gurkhas – originally the men of Gorkha, a tiny mountainous kingdom to the west of Kathmandu – unified the plethora of principalities, chiefdoms and statelets into what is now Nepal. Then they looked east and marched into Sikkim; they looked west and conquered Garhwal; they even invaded Tibet and for a time extracted tribute from the Emperor of China, before being pushed back into their mountain stronghold. Now they cast their eyes south to the Plain of Bengal, to what seemed a land rich beyond the dreams of mere soldiers, where the streets were paved with gold, the women and the cattle were fat, a man only had to throw a seed onto the ground for it to grow, and the people were seemingly indolent and unwarlike. Inevitably this brought them into conflict with the British, in the form of the East India Company, which, no longer primarily a trading organisation, governed huge tracts of British India. The Company also had an army, composed of locally raised regiments of native soldiers with British officers and regiments of the British Army stationed in India but paid for by the Company.

The Anglo-Nepal War of 1814 to 1816 was hard-fought and bloody. The British had been accustomed to turning up, firing a disciplined volley or two, and seeing vastly larger native hordes break and run. The Gurkhas too had grown used to dispersing numerically superior enemies by a ferocious but controlled charge. Neither side would run away, to the consternation of the other. Technology favoured the British, while geography was on the side of the Gurkhas.

Unusually for the time and place, both sides treated prisoners honourably, controlled looting and behaved properly towards civilians and women. A mutual respect grew up between the adversaries. In November 1814, at Kalunga, a Gurkha army under General Balbahadur was surrounded and cut off by a British force. Eventually Balbahadur's men ran out of food, water and ammunition, but still they would not surrender. Drawing their kukris, they chanced all on one last charge straight towards the besieging British. They were mown down in their hundreds and only a very few got away. After the battle the British raised two identical monuments, which stand at Kalunga to this day. One is to the fallen British soldiers, the other 'to our gallant adversary' who 'fought in their conflict like men'.

When the war ended in stalemate, the Company concluded that the Gurkhas had been the toughest opponent it had yet faced in the east and that it would be better by far to have them as friends, fighting for the British rather than against them. The King of Nepal and his advisers agreed – they now had a very large number of fit young men, with no means

Exemplary loyalty, courage and skill: Gurkhas marching in formation in India

of employing them. If the British wanted them as soldiers, then let them have them – and anyway, the Nepali rulers rather liked the British.

The first British Gurkha battalion was raised from Gurkha prisoners of war in British hands, and while it was part of the British Indian Army it was obvious from the early days that Gurkhas were different. They were nominally Hindu, but not obsessively so: they were unconcerned by rules of caste and what could or could not be eaten; they liked strong drink; and they had a British sense of humour. When the Indian Mutiny broke out in 1857 the Gurkhas were the first non-British troops to go into action against the mutineers, and their loyalty was never in doubt.

The mutiny put down, Gurkhas, like other loyal races, were rewarded, and by the outbreak of World War I there were ten regiments of Gurkhas, each with two battalions. Six Gurkha battalions fought on the Western Front, others at Gallipoli and in Mesopotamia and Palestine. In addition to the 20,000 Gurkhas already serving in 1914, a further 55,000 volunteered during the war, and the Nepal army was put at the disposal of the British. Between 1914 and 1918 almost every Gurkha of military age was serving the British, and of those who joined the British Gurkha regiments one in ten was killed – a higher proportion even than the British. In World War II around 150,000 Gurkhas served, fighting in Burma, North Africa and Italy. Again, ten per cent were killed.

After Indian independence in 1947, the Brigade of Gurkhas was divided between the new Indian and the British armies. To Britain came four battalions of infantry, each with two battalions, and subsequently new regiments of engineers, signals and transport were raised. The Brigade was given little time to settle down, however, for the Malayan Emergency broke out in June 1948, and the battle against Communist terrorists was to be the major focus for the Gurkhas until the final defeat of the insurgency in 1960.

In 1962 came the Brunei revolt and 'Konfrontasi', an attempt by Indonesia to seize the British colonies and protectorates in north Borneo and prevent the formation of Malaysia. Gurkhas formed the nucleus of the British force, and when in 1967 Indonesia acknowledged defeat, the campaign was rightly held up as an example of cost-effective professionalism. It was during the Borneo campaign that, in November 1965, the first Victoria Cross to be awarded since the Korean War was won by a Gurkha, Lance Corporal Rambahadur Limbu. Rambahadur's son is, at the time of writing, a Gurkha officer and second-in-command of the Demonstration Company at the Royal Military Academy, Sandhurst.

Then came reductions in the armed forces as a whole, and a decision by the British government to reduce its presence in the Far East. Soon the five remaining Gurkha battalions were spread between Hong Kong, Brunei and the United Kingdom. It was the UK Gurkha battalion that was deployed to Cyprus in 1974 and to the Falklands War in 1982. The ending of the Cold War and the handing over of Hong Kong to Communist China brought further cuts in the British armed forces, and the Gurkhas, with no members of Parliament and no county connections to lobby for them, were cut by nearly 70 per cent

Arakan, January 1944: a Gurkha carrying a wounded comrade, photographed by Cecil Beaton

during the 'Options for Change' exercise in the mid 1990s. Today the British Army has two battalions of Gurkha infantry, two squadrons each of Gurkha engineer, signals and logistic troops, demonstration companies at Sandhurst and the Infantry Training Centre, and a recruit training company – about 3,500 Gurkhas in total.

Every year, beginning in November, recruiting for the Brigade starts in Nepal. Around 60,000 young men come forward for the 300 or so places available, and in January those selected after rigorous tests of mental and physical stamina, intelligence and capacity to learn are flown to England to begin their 40-week recruit training programme at Catterick, where Gurkha officers and NCOs will prepare them to take their place in the modern British Army. The recruit training period for Gurkhas is longer than that of their British contemporaries, for they must learn not only to be soldiers, but also to fit into a world of electricity, running water, motor cars, computers, railways and aircraft. The Gurkha's minimum period of service, however, is 15 years, compared to an average of around four years for British soldiers.

On completion of recruit training, and trade training for soldiers going to the technical corps of the Brigade, the young Gurkhas join their regiments. Promotion is dependent upon merit, service and qualification, and competition is fierce. A small number of British officers – around 12 in a battalion, compared to over 30 in a British equivalent – hold the more senior posts, while platoon commanders and company seconds-in-command are Gurkha officers, men who have joined as young recruits and have worked their way up the ranks. British officers in Gurkha units are required to be fluent speakers of Nepali – the language used within Gurkha units – and to be conversant with all aspects of their men's culture, religion and homeland.

It is sometimes suggested that the very existence of the Brigade of Gurkhas in the British Army is an anachronism in the 21st century, but there is nothing wrong with an anachronism provided that it works, and provided that it is freely entered into by both sides. By any objective standards of military competence – annual shooting results, physical fitness tests, retention figures and disciplinary statistics – Gurkhas are amongst the best soldiers anywhere in the world. By their record of exemplary loyalty, courage and skill, Gurkhas have earned their place in the British Army, and they will keep it for as long as they remain cost-effective and maintain the highest standards of professional excellence. Recent experience in Kosovo, East Timor, Afghanistan and Iraq shows that they are doing just that.

The Home Guard
Jimmy Perry

When the lads of the village get cracking
And the whole platoon turns out,
Off we go, rain or snow,
Just like proper soldiers, all in a row.

These are the words of a hit song of 1941 by the famous comedian George Formby. The 'proper soldiers' he referred to were the Home Guard. As a young man of 17, I used to sing this along with my comrades on route marches. We didn't mind that people made jokes about it. In spite of the words 'Home Guard' on our battle-dress shoulders, we *were* proper soldiers.

Within a few minutes of war being declared, on 3 September 1939, the air raid sirens sounded. Everyone in Britain had expected terrible air raids. They'd seen it so often on newsreels of the Spanish Civil War and they'd also seen the film *Things to Come*, based on the story by H. G. Wells, in which London was destroyed by air raids in a matter of hours; so when the sirens sounded, it was only to be expected. However, it turned out to be a false alarm: not a single German plane appeared; in fact *nothing* happened. It was the start of the so-called Phoney War. Theatres and cinemas that had closed when war was declared started to open again. In France British and French troops manned the 'impregnable' Maginot Line, and there were newsreel shots of French troops being taught how to play cricket by our Tommies. After a month or two of anxiety, the country settled down to a wartime winter.

As winter gave way to spring, the lull was suddenly shattered when the whole might of the German army attacked, not the Maginot Line the British and French troops were manning, but through Belgium. Unfortunately, the Maginot Line stopped at the frontier, so the Germans simply went round the side. As one British MP remarked in the House of Commons, 'It was a typical shabby Nazi trick'. Within a few weeks the French had surrendered and the British were forced to evacuate from Dunkirk. Britain stood alone.

On 23 July the Home Guard was born. Earlier, in May, when the Germans were advancing on all fronts, the War Minister, Anthony Eden, made his historic broadcast calling for volunteers between the ages of 17 and 65 to come forward to defend the homeland. Within a week a quarter of a million men had enrolled. A large number of them were veterans of World War I. At first they were known as the LDV (Local Defence Volunteers), but Churchill insisted that the name be changed to the Home Guard. Anything that could be used as a weapon was pressed into service – old rifles, shotguns, pikes, swords, petrol bombs.

Overleaf: *The inspiration for Jimmy Perry's* Dad's Army: *the Home Guard in training, 1940*

I was 16 and wanted to enrol at once, but my dear mother, whose two brothers had been seriously wounded in World War I, was horrified at the thought of my being in uniform.

At last the day came when I reached the official age of 17, and I volunteered. When it was first formed the Home Guard had no uniforms and was terribly short of weapons and equipment, but in spite of this it fulfilled a desperate need; people could see that *something* was being done to protect Britain. Within a year the whole scene had changed: President Roosevelt had sent two ships loaded with rifles – true, they had equipped the American army in World War I, but they were a godsend. Although over 30 years old, they were very efficient .300 calibre Ross rifles, accurate and with magazines that held five rounds. Roosevelt also sent quite a number of Thompson sub-machine-guns that held either a clip of bullets or a drum which contained 50 rounds. All of us boys had seen them in American gangster films and were thrilled when we first handled them. By the time I joined, nearly a year after its formation, the Home Guard was a well-equipped force of over two million men.

And so I became a member of the Watford Company of the Home Guard of the Beds and Herts Regiment. Members of various units all over the country wore the cap badges of the local regiment. In *Dad's Army*, because the fictitious town of Warmington on Sea was in Kent, the platoon wore the cap badge of the Royal West Kents.

The training was mostly based on guerrilla tactics. Quite a number of the officers had experienced the slaughter in the trenches of World War I, and 'Colonel Blimp' tactics, as they were referred to, were definitely out. (Colonel Blimp was a cartoon character, created by David Lowe, which represented the old-fashioned type of reactionary army officer.) In our unit there were men who had served with the International Brigade during the Spanish Civil War, and we learned what modern warfare was all about. As time went by, most of the older men, who had been in from the start, were weeded out or given admin jobs, which they deeply resented. We young boys were glad, as we felt they were holding us back, especially on manoeuvres when they just couldn't keep up. Our commanding officer, the manager of a building society, had to relinquish his command due to his age, and a younger man was appointed. I took to the training like a duck to water, and after a very few weeks was issued with my own personal rifle, with strict instructions to keep it by me at all times. But we youngsters were not issued with ammunition; if we heard the church bells – which was the signal that the Germans had invaded – our instructions were to jump on our bikes, pedal furiously to our headquarters, and draw our 50 rounds of ammunition.

Our new CO decided to form a special commando unit that was composed only of us teenagers. A new badge was designed in the form of a large 'C', which we wore on our shoulders. This invited ribald comments from kids, but we wore it with pride. Our enthusiasm knew no limits. We were constantly devising new weapons – wire cheese-cutters to creep up behind German sentries and decapitate them, sharpened bicycle chains for close combat – and I wore my Boy Scout knife, which had been honed to razor sharpness; all this topped off with our rifles and bayonet. Our training never stopped, and took the form of competitions: two teams would strip down and reassemble Lewis guns blindfolded. We prided ourselves on our drill, which we practised constantly.

Every month there would be a special week – Dig for Victory Week, Buy a Spitfire Week, Red Cross Week, and many others – and to start it off there would be a parade, usually on a Saturday. Watford had a new town hall, a magnificent building that had only been completed a few weeks before war broke out; in front, a large podium was erected and the mayor and local dignitaries, along with some rather ancient senior service officers, took the salute. All branches of civil defence wanted to take part in the parade: ARP, fire service, ambulance, land girls, nurses – it was endless. But we boys of the Watford Home Guard Commando Unit always led it, with the Sea Scouts Bugle and Drum Band. There was constant rivalry between the Home Guard and the ARP wardens, but we always won: our drill was so smart and the wardens', because they wore soft shoes, was rotten.

Another vital part of our training was unarmed combat: how to deal with an attacker with a knife; how to deal with someone who attacked you from behind (run your boot down his shin and stamp hard on his foot). This was all very violent, but the whole country was geared up not to give, or expect, any quarter: we were fighting for our lives. There was a film made in 1942, which is shown quite often on television, called *Went the Day Well?* It was a propaganda film, but it gives a very accurate picture of life at that time and the role of the Home Guard features strongly.

Something very few people know about the Home Guard is that it took over quite a few police duties. Because so many police had been drafted into the forces, their work was being done by special constables, of whom there were still not enough. So when we were on duty we stopped suspicious-looking characters and asked to see their identity cards. This did not go down very well with the general public, especially factory workers returning home after a ten-hour shift to be confronted by a young boy with a rifle and fixed bayonet demanding to see their identification.

The Home Guard never had to face the enemy, but with weapons in over two million households there were bound to be accidents, and sadly, on manoeuvres, quite a few men were killed. The Home Guard played a very important part in the war effort, amongst many other things guarding vital installations, thus releasing the regular army for service overseas. In January 1944 I was called up into the regular army, the Royal Artillery, and I became a 'proper soldier'; but I shall always be proud to have been a member of Britain's Home Guard.

The Charge of the Light Brigade
Keith Lowe

At first glance it is difficult to see why the Charge of the Light Brigade should be celebrated as a great episode in our history. For the past 150 years it has been remembered as one of the British Army's biggest blunders: the moment when a botched order during the battle of Balaclava sent more than 600 cavalrymen to face the full force of the Russian artillery with little but their sabres to defend themselves. In a war marked by catastrophic British mistakes, when thousands of soldiers would die of cold, hunger and disease because of a lack of even basic supplies, this episode still stands out as exceptional in its sheer wastefulness of human life. And yet it is impossible not to admire the bravery of the officers and men who entered what Tennyson was to immortalise as the 'valley of Death' on that October morning in 1854. In the entire history of warfare, there are few blunders quite so heroic, or quite so glorious, as the Charge of the Light Brigade.

The episode took place at the height of the Crimean War, when the British and French armies had just begun their year-long siege of Sevastopol. As the allies dug in around the city, the Russian field army did not try to dislodge them. Instead they marched on the British supply base, 15 miles away at Balaclava. The idea was that if they could break through the allied regiments and seize the port then the entire British Army would be cut off from their supplies. Without food, clothing and ammunition, the British besiegers would be forced to surrender.

The Russians marched on Balaclava with 25,000 foot soldiers and six massive formations of horsemen – more than twice the number of men and horses available to the British Commander-in-Chief, Lord Raglan. Very soon they had occupied a valley just north of the port and had driven Raglan's Turkish allies from their strongholds on the high ground along the valley's side. After some desperate skirmishing, which saved Balaclava from complete disaster, Raglan saw an opportunity to counterattack and drive the Russians back. Accordingly, he ordered his cavalry to move forward and 'recover the Heights' on the right-hand side of the valley.

Unfortunately the British cavalry commander, Lord Lucan, misinterpreted Raglan's orders and dithered at the valley's mouth. Raglan watched him from a nearby plateau with increasing frustration, wondering when he was going to attack. After about half an hour the Russians finally realised that they were overexposed and started preparing to remove all the Turkish guns they had captured and retreat to safer positions. Seeing this, Raglan was incensed that the opportunity to save their valuable artillery was about to be lost. He sent down a second order to Lucan, which read: 'Lord Raglan wishes the cavalry to advance rapidly to the front, and try to prevent the enemy carrying away the guns … Immediate.'

If Lord Lucan was able to misinterpret Raglan's first, fairly specific order, then the vagueness of this second order would prove catastrophic. From where he was standing

Lucan could not see the Turkish redoubts on the right-hand side of the valley, or the guns that were about to be carried away – in fact, the only guns he could see were the main Russian battery, at the end of the valley, which were pointing directly towards them. He promptly denounced Raglan's orders as useless and dangerous, but the messenger was adamant: the cavalry must attack immediately.

Still in disbelief, Lucan passed the order on to the leader of the Light Brigade, Lord Cardigan. Cardigan was equally incredulous, and is reputed to have said: 'There must be some mistake. I shall never be able to bring a single man back.' 'I cannot help that,' Lucan replied. 'It is Lord Raglan's positive order that the Light Brigade attacks immediately.'

Not wishing to appear cowardly, Cardigan promptly rode back to the head of his brigade and prepared to lead them into battle – not towards the escaping Turkish guns on the ridge, as Raglan had intended, but straight into the mouths of the amassed Russian artillery at the other end of the valley. Up on the plateau, Raglan and his staff watched in horror as the 673 men and horses of the Light Brigade took off in completely the wrong direction. 'We could scarcely believe the evidence of our senses,' wrote William Howard Russell, the correspondent for *The Times*. 'Surely that handful of men were not going to charge an army in position?'

The Light Brigade did exactly that. Not only were they faced by the head-on fire of the whole Russian army, they were also exposed to fire from the Russian-held hills on their left and the captured Turkish redoubts on their right. As they rode forward at a trot, the first men began to fall under the Russian musket-fire, including the brigade's trumpeter who was killed just after giving the signal for them to gallop. Undeterred, the rest rode on. Even when the artillery on their flanks opened up, littering the plain with the bodies of dying men and horses, they continued to gallop forward towards the end of the valley, where the polished brass of the Russian cannon was waiting for them, glinting in the autumn sunlight.

When the main battery finally opened up, the effect was devastating. The Russian shells blew whole sections of the front line to pieces. Many of those who were not hit found themselves drenched in the blood of their comrades, as the ground was torn up beneath them and their bodies rent to pieces. And yet, above the din of the guns, the squadrons could still hear Cardigan's voice calling them to remain steady. As the cannon let out one final salvo at point blank range, the few men who still lived raised their swords above their heads with a flash of steel and began their final charge upon their enemy.

The miracle of this episode is that any of the cavalrymen made it to the Russian lines at all. Of the 300 men in the front line of the Brigade, only 30 managed to approach the battery head on. Some had been pushed out to the sides by the force of the artillery bombardment, but most had been blown off their horses. At the head of the surviving few, Lord Cardigan leapt between two cannon on his horse and was immediately set upon by the waiting Cossacks. Since Cardigan considered it improper for a gentleman to participate in the actual cut and thrust of battle personally, it is remarkable that he managed to survive.

Overleaf: *Into the valley of Death:* The Charge of the Light Brigade *by R. Caton Woodville*

As the rest of the men rallied to him, the survivors of the second line arrived and began to overturn the Russian cannon. The impossible had happened: the Light Brigade had broken through and were causing havoc in the Russian lines.

For a while they pressed home their attack, armed only with their swords and their mind-boggling courage, but their situation was plainly hopeless. Before them stood the combined mass of 25,000 Russian soldiers, and behind them some 500 Russian lancers were closing off their route of escape. In desperation, they left off the fight and turned to ride back the way they had come, harried by the same rifle-fire they had encountered on the way in. When they approached the Russian lancers who barred their retreat, the Light Brigade began their second charge of the day, this time in a desperate bid to escape. As one of them later recalled, they smashed through the ranks of Russian horsemen 'as if they had been made of tinsel paper'.

Of the 673 men who set out at the beginning, only 176 returned on their horses. Though many others made their way back later on foot, or were brought back wounded, the scale of the losses in the front line was stupefying. The 13th Light Dragoons, which had numbered 150 just an hour before, could now muster only 14 men. Up on the plateau, many of the spectators were reduced to silent tears as they watched the remnants of the Light Brigade return. The French general Pierre Bosquet, who had witnessed the whole event, muttered a fitting epitaph: 'It is magnificent,' he said, 'but it is not war.'

Long after the Crimean War was over, recriminations as to who was responsible for the errors that had led to the terrible slaughter at Balaclava still flew. Some blamed Lucan for not paying proper attention to Raglan's original orders; others blamed Raglan himself, or his messenger. Even Cardigan did not escape criticism for leading his men so readily to their deaths, though he dined out on the story of his survival for the rest of his life. The only thing that was never called into question was the astonishing courage of the soldiers involved. The Charge of the Light Brigade was a horrendous blunder, but it showed the Russians that, for bravery and sheer bloody-mindedness, the British cavalryman had no equal. One hundred and fifty years on the event is still remembered as the worst kind of military failure, because it was so completely unnecessary. And yet we can rightly feel proud of the gallant men who fell in that valley. They are the embodiment of a principle that would be proved time and again throughout our history, that even when the British fail, and fail spectacularly, they do so with a dignity and a devotion to duty that is truly heroic.

The longbows of Agincourt
Robert Hardy

'Be it thy cause to busy giddy minds with foreign quarrels,' says Shakespeare's Henry IV to his son Hal, who was to become Henry V, the victor of Agincourt – the best known and best documented battle of the Hundred Years War. As so often, Shakespeare has his finger on the pulse of history, and in his *Henry V* the new young King says:

> I will keep my state,
> Be like a king and show my sail of greatness
> When I do rouse me in my throne of France!

Claiming that throne, as his great-grandfather Edward III had done, Henry Plantagenet invaded France just two years after his coronation, laying siege to Harfleur on 18 August 1415. With him were 2,000 knights and men-at-arms, 8,000 longbowmen and 65 gunners. There were priests and cooks, sappers and pioneers, farriers, painters, armourers, tentmakers, bowyers and fletchers, masons, cordwainers, carters, turners and carpenters. There were dukes at a daily rate of thirteen shillings and fourpence; earls at six and eightpence; barons at four shillings; knights, esquires and men-at-arms at two shillings, one-and-sixpence, and a shilling respectively. The thousands of longbowmen were paid a new rate of sixpence a day.

The siege lasted well into September, and by the time the town surrendered, war, heat, desertion and disease had taken a rough toll of Henry's army. His war council advised him to call it a day, go home, raise more money and troops and continue the campaign in the spring, but an almost mystical belief in his destiny determined him to overrule them and march to English-held Calais, some 150 miles to the north, through hostile territory. Such was his faith in himself and his archers – his 'yew hedge' he called them – that the depleted army marched out of the north gate of Harfleur on 8 October.

We can be pretty sure of the numbers that accompanied Henry: his chaplain counted 900 knights and men-at-arms and 5,000 archers, marching through Normandy in unseasonably bad weather to a very uncertain future, but held in the hand of an inspired leader. Their hope of crossing the Somme by the ford through which Edward III's army had fought its way before Crécy disappeared when they found it blocked and heavily guarded, and for the next week the drenched and tattered army moved eastwards, feeling for a crossing, which they eventually found on the 19th. There followed another week of marching north-west in appalling weather, dogged by the French, whose massive and ominous tracks they came upon in the mud, crossing their line of march.

On the 24th they reached a little river, the Ternoise at Blangy, and pushed up the steep incline beyond it. A scout came spurring back, and as each contingent reached the top they saw the vast army of the French moving slowly up the open valley to their right. Henry drew

up his army for battle, but in the fading October light the French moved on behind the woods until they reappeared ahead, right across the road to Calais through the flat country between the villages of Maisoncelles, Tramecourt and Azincourt: three great masses of men and horses, gleaming with armour and lances, forested with bright heraldic banners – 'in multitudes compared with us,' said the chaplain, 'an innumerable host of locusts'. Henry heard Sir Walter Hungerford say he wished they had 'ten thousand more good English archers, who would gladly have been there'. Henry replied: 'You speak as a fool … I would not have one more even if I could … The God of Heaven … can bring down the pride of these Frenchmen, who so boast of their numbers and their strength.'

On the morning of 25 October, St Crispin's Day, the two armies drew up for battle, the giant and the dwarf, the disproportion estimated at anything between three to one and ten to one. The three masses of the French were crowded one behind the other; the English had 6,000 men on a front of approximately 1,000 yards, the 900 lances in three small battalions – 'battles' – four men deep, the much greater force of archers between them and on their flanks. The movement of either army was limited by the woods of Tramecourt to the east and Azincourt to the west.

Argument continues as to the exact formation of the archers: two contemporaries who were there speak of them being 'in two wings' and 'at the two sides of the men-at-arms'; while the chaplain, sitting on his horse to the rear, says they were 'in blocks (or wedges) intermixed with each battalion'. What is certain is that they must, however placed, have occupied much more ground than the men-at-arms, and that they would have been positioned so as to have their whole front, and the enemy's, within their shooting range – about 300 to 350 yards.

No doubt they were a raggedy mob to look at, those 5,000 archers, but they represented a broad cross-section of the tough rural population of England and Wales. They were men used to living by physical labour and the strength of their bodies – a strength developed from their early years, through practice enforced by statute, into great skill with the longbow. At Agincourt that strength and ability were goaded into supreme action by despair. They were up against fearful odds, yet somehow their extraordinary leader kept them together and summoned their spirit for them. Henry had also told them the French would cut off the drawing fingers of every archer captured. They meant to die hard. They were sure of their familiar weapons, heavy yew longbows which could shoot mail- and plate-piercing war arrows at a minimum rate of ten arrows a minute. (Five thousand men shooting – do the sums!) If the weapons found in the Tudor *Mary Rose* were typical of those used 130 years earlier, these longbows would have had a draw-weight ranging from 100 to 170 pounds, which the archer would have had to hold briefly at an average full draw of some 30 inches – and this after a march of 260 miles in 17 days with only one day's rest.

Since crossing the Somme, each archer had carried a pointed stake, which on this morning of battle he drove into the soft ground before him, angled breast-high towards

Henry V's 'yew hedge': the longbows of Agincourt in Laurence Olivier's 1944 film

the enemy. Onto those pointed stakes the French flank cavalry lumbered through the mud and the huzzing arrow storm until, maddened with pain, the survivors plunged back into the front line which was advancing on foot behind them, funnelling into the narrowing space between the woods where Henry had established his final line. When the armies crashed together and the archers could no longer shoot, they abandoned bows and quivers and went in with sword and maul, dagger and war-hammer, mounting on the growing piles of French dead to strike at those below who came on into the shambles, pressed by the thousands still behind them. As one French writer put it: 'the superiority of the English archers rested in their ability to transform themselves in an instant into men-at-arms … French archers could do nothing beyond drawing their bows.'

After the battle, the exhausted, triumphant army slept where they had the night before. In the morning, they marched through the heaps of stripped dead (between 6,000 and 10,000 of them), and as they passed the files of French prisoners it is said that they mockingly held up the first two fingers of their right hands – their drawing fingers – thus, if the story is true, giving birth to the V-sign. St Crispin's had been a monstrous day but, at the end of it, it was to the ordinary men of England, the yeomen of the shires and their many Welsh colleagues, with their simple longbow and their giant spirit, that the victory of Agincourt belonged.

The relief of Mafeking
Ian Knight

On the evening of 16 May 1900 the vanguard of a British relief column rode into the dusty
South African town of Mafeking. They had been a long time coming: for 217 days the
garrison of Mafeking had been besieged by the Boers. Yet, to their surprise, the first man
they met reacted to the prospect of relief with a whimsy which typifies the Mafeking saga:
'Oh yes,' he said, 'I heard you were knocking about.'

If the besieged reacted coolly enough to their salvation, however, Great Britain as a
whole did not. For six months Mafeking had been a symbol of hope and endurance, and
when news of the relief broke in London there were spontaneous celebrations in the streets.
The mood of public euphoria continued for a week – 'the most wonderful and harmless
saturnalia of the century', according to one reporter – and added a new verb to the
dictionary, coined specifically to describe it: to *maffick*.

Mafeking itself was an unlikely spot to attract such rapture. No more than a station-
stop on the railway line from Kimberley to Rhodesia (now Zimbabwe), it was, according
to the commander of the British garrison there, Colonel Robert Baden-Powell, 'just a small
tin-roofed town of small houses plumped down upon the open veldt'. Even before the
outbreak of the Anglo-Boer War in 1899, however, its history had been turbulent. More
correctly known as Mafikeng – 'the place of stones' – it had been a major settlement of
the Tsidi Rolong section of the Tswana people for centuries. During the 1880s the Tswana
had been the subject of freebooting expeditions by the Boers, who played one chieftain
off against another to win land. The British had intervened and annexed the area as
Bechuanaland, and an administrative capital of sorts had been established close by the
African town of Mafikeng.

In 1899 Mafeking – as the whites called it – was home to about 1,700 Europeans and
perhaps 5,000 Africans. The town had little enough strategic significance – certainly
nothing to compare with Ladysmith or Kimberley – and indeed, had the Boers captured the
whole of the Kimberley–Rhodesia railway when war broke out in October 1899 it would
have made little difference to the course of the fighting. Yet from the first Mafeking achieved
a symbolic significance that far outweighed its military importance. Its name was already
inextricably entwined in the history of Anglo-Boer rivalry, for in 1895 Dr Jameson had
begun his famous and abortive raid on Johannesburg – an attempt to overthrow the Boer
government in the Transvaal by an armed coup – from a base near Mafeking. Moreover, the
town represented one step on the great imperial dream of the age, the British hope to link
the length of Africa – Cape to Cairo – with a railway. If Mafeking fell to the Boers, it would
represent more than anything a blow to imperial self-confidence in southern Africa.

Baden-Powell instinctively understood that appearances would be as important to his
war as ground lost or won. He had been sent to Mafeking in the tense months before the

war to raise a volunteer regiment to protect the Bechuanaland borders, and found himself occupying the town with just 20 officers and 680 men.

The story of Mafeking during the Anglo-Boer War is essentially the story of Baden-Powell, in all his complexity. In his early forties, nearly bald, dapper, with a brisk and breezy manner and a penchant for amateur theatricals, B-P – as he was universally known – was no stranger to southern Africa. His experiences in Zululand in 1888 and Rhodesia in 1896 had revealed a tendency to approach war as a Boys' Own adventure. He was a keen advocate of the importance of scouting, an enthusiasm that had not been diminished by an unfortunate incident in Zululand when he had got lost while trying to identify a hostile stronghold and had attacked a friendly group of Zulus by mistake. No sooner had he arrived in Mafeking than he applied his considerable energy to the question of its defence.

There is no doubt that this was necessary, for during the first few weeks of the war the Boer general Piet Cronje moved over 6,000 men to take the town. B-P resolutely stuck to his guns, however, and in many ways this was his greatest achievement of the war. By drawing off a portion of the Boer armies at a time when such numbers might have made a crucial difference elsewhere he undoubtedly helped the overall British war effort. After a month, however, Cronje decided Mafeking was not worth it and moved elsewhere, leaving a much smaller force to invest the town.

It was at this point that the siege assumed its true character. The Boers shelled the town regularly, causing few European casualties but steadily knocking the buildings to pieces. Occasionally they would try to rush one of B-P's outlying positions; occasionally B-P would make a foray to 'kick' them back. For the most part the siege was dreary and onerous, although the infrequent skirmishes were intense enough to add a very real frisson of danger.

B-P relished his role and assumed a manner of jaunty defiance which was as essential to Mafeking's survival as was the rather more steely determination that underpinned it. He recorded the first Boer bombardment with a despatch which read: 'All well. Four hours bombardment. One dog killed.' Chronically short of men and equipment, he improvised new ways of prosecuting the defence. Ancient cannon were pressed into service to augment his meagre supply of artillery, an armoured train chugged along the few miles of track left undamaged by the Boers to make sorties, and hand-grenades made from jam-tins were delivered into Boer positions by a champion bowler. Equally important were his efforts to keep up morale inside the town. He organised race meetings and gymkhanas, and when money ran short he printed his own siege currency, with his face on the notes. Africans were encouraged to display the collective contempt for Boer shelling by picking up dud shells and selling them as souvenirs. B-P himself was a dynamo, always light-hearted and cheerily optimistic, and tackled the siege as if it were a cricket match, to be played to the full. In this he was assisted by a number of journalists who, cooped up in the town with little to write about for long periods, found good copy in B-P's antics. When reports of brave little Mafeking's stand reached the outside world they caught the public imagination, the more so

A triumph of 'British pluck and valour': news of the relief of Mafeking reaches London

because British fortunes elsewhere in the war at the time were decidedly mixed.

Yet there was also a dark side to the siege. Lying so close to the white settlement, the African town at Mafeking had been incorporated within B-P's defence perimeter, and in his treatment of the Africans B-P revealed a ruthless streak. He regarded them as a resource like any other, to be used or discarded for the betterment of the white inhabitants. At a time in the war when both sides shied away from arming Africans B-P distributed arms to the Rolong, and allowed them not only to defend themselves against Boer attacks but to raid Boer lines for provisions – an act which aroused Cronje's indignation:

> It is understood you have armed Bastards, Fingos and Baralongs against us – in this you have committed an enormous act of wickedness … reconsider the matter, even if it cost you the loss of Mafeking … disarm your blacks and thereby act the part of a white man in a white man's war.

B-P did not disarm them; when they were useful he used them, and when their usefulness was done he discarded them. Rations for black Africans were cut to safeguard food for the whites, a decision which caused immense hardship. No protection was provided against shellfire in the African town, and over 300 were killed during the course of the siege. As it progressed, and B-P fretted about his supplies, he ordered hundreds of Africans to be driven away from the town. Many were shot by the Boers, who did not want them either; others returned to the British positions having been stripped and flogged.

With the British preoccupied with the sieges of Ladysmith and Kimberley, the siege of Mafeking dragged on. An early attempt to relieve the town by a march from Rhodesia was checked by the Boers. Yet by the beginning of May 1900 the tide was turning. The other sieges were lifted, and Johannesburg had fallen to the British. In the beginning of May a fresh attempt was made to fight a way through to Mafeking. The Boers, of course, saw it coming, and made one last determined effort to breach B-P's defences. An attack penetrated B-P's blind spot, the African settlement, and had almost reached the European town before it was checked. The Boers surrendered rather than face the wrath of the irate Rolong.

The main body of the relief column entered Mafeking on 17 May 1900. Their arrival changed little in the broader course of the war, but within hours of the news reaching London by telegram, crowds thronged the streets singing 'God Save the Queen' and 'Rule Britannia'; church bells rang, fireworks were let off and bonfires lit, and policemen sent to keep a watchful eye were deliriously kissed. The relief of Mafeking was a reaffirmation of the British spirit – as the Lord Mayor of London proudly proclaimed, it proved that 'British pluck and valour, when used in the right cause, must triumph'. Around the Empire, from Canada to New Zealand, the reaction was much the same. Robert Baden-Powell emerged from the Anglo-Boer War not only as one of the few high-ranking British officers to have their reputations enhanced, but as a genuine public hero. If the remainder of his military career would prove undistinguished, he was at least able to use his experiences and his influence to create the Boy Scout movement.

The Duke of Marlborough
Charles Spencer

John Churchill, 1st Duke of Marlborough, was born in 1650, the son of an impoverished
Royalist cavalier. He rose to lead the soldiers of the Grand Alliance against Louis XIV in the
War of the Spanish Succession (1702–12). The path of his career was dependent on royal
favour, a fickle source of power for a startling, consistent talent: this was a general who never
lost a battle, or failed successfully to complete a siege.

Educated at St Paul's in London, John followed his father, Winston, into the royal
household. Churchill's first patron was the Duke of York, the future James II. In 1667, while
watching a military display in London, the Duke of York turned to his page boy and asked
him what he would most like in the world. 'A pair of colours,' came the reply – a dream that
became reality when the 16-year-old was given an ensign's commission in the King's Own
Company of Foot Guards. Between 1668 and 1671 Churchill was posted to Tangiers, where
he fought the Moors.

As a young man Churchill enjoyed a passionate affair with Barbara Castlemaine,
Charles II's most promiscuous mistress. Smitten by her young and handsome lover – she
was a decade his senior – Castlemaine gave Churchill £5,000, the cornerstone of his future
power and wealth at a time when court and military positions were tradeable commodities.

In May 1672 Churchill fought alongside the Duke of York at Sole Bay, a bruising battle
between the English and Dutch fleets. Churchill acquitted himself with sufficient distinction
to merit a double promotion to a captaincy of marines.

1673 saw Churchill serving in the Royal English Regiment, for the French and against
the Dutch. Louis XIV was an enthusiastic spectator at the siege of Maastricht, where he
witnessed Churchill save the Duke of Monmouth's life and rebuff a doomed Dutch
counteroffensive. Louis personally thanked the English captain for his efforts, and wrote
to Charles II recommending him for further promotion. This was an act of patronage that
the Sun King was greatly to regret.

Churchill's apprenticeship was completed in 1674–5 under Turenne, perhaps the
greatest of Louis XIV's marshals. Turenne's dictum was: 'Make few sieges and fight plenty
of battles; when you are master of the countryside the villages will give us the town.' An
indication of how profoundly Turenne's creed influenced Churchill can be seen in his
statement in later life that winning a battle was 'of far greater advantage to the common
cause than the taking of twenty towns'. Audacity was to be Churchill's hallmark.

Returning to London, Churchill met a teenaged maid of honour, Sarah Jenyns. The
daughter of impoverished Hertfordshire gentry, Sarah was a feisty beauty. Churchill was
captivated by her, and she found John 'as handsome as an angel'. The couple married
quietly in the winter of 1677–8. Sarah brought as her dowry the adoring friendship of
Princess Anne, the Duke of York's younger daughter. This slow, unprepossessing, lonely

girl would one day be Queen of England. Churchill's marriage to Anne's great confidante was to define the remainder of his career. In 1683 Princess Anne set up her own court, with Sarah Churchill at its hub.

Charles II's death in 1685 brought James II to the throne. In the first year of his reign the Duke of Monmouth invaded, and Churchill quickly moved to the south-west to harry him before he could settle. After a disappointing campaign, Monmouth ordered a desperate night attack on the royal army at Sedgemoor. Although nominally second-in-command, it was Churchill who oversaw the destruction of Monmouth's army.

A devout Protestant, Churchill was alienated by his monarch's increasingly brazen championing of Catholicism, which even saw papists appointed as army officers. When William of Orange invaded England in 1688, Churchill rode over to his cause, deserting the man who had ensured his rise from obscurity.

William III's relationship with Churchill was uneven. Although grateful for his role in the Glorious Revolution, for which Churchill was rewarded with the earldom of Marlborough, William was wary of the smooth and enigmatic soldier-courtier. In 1689 Marlborough impressed at the battle of Walcourt: he was at the head of the cavalry charge that decided the day. Two years later, Marlborough led a masterful attack on the Irish ports of Cork and Kinsale, capturing two of the exiled James II's remaining strongholds in Ireland. By contrast, William III was an unsuccessful soldier. It is probable that he envied Marlborough's gifts.

Marlborough was a covert correspondent with the Jacobites in St Germain, no doubt insuring against a second Stuart restoration. He was also frustrated by William's increasing reliance on Dutch and German generals, which stymied his own, intense, ambition. In 1692 Marlborough was dismissed from his posts and committed to the Tower. Although found innocent of the charges, it is likely that Marlborough was one of several sources who betrayed the British invasion of Brest in 1694, which resulted in severe casualties.

At the end of the 1690s William knew his own health was waning, and he could foresee the eminence of the Marlboroughs in the next reign. The Earl was the one man who could guarantee that England contributed to the alliance needed to block Louis XIV's European ambitions. Before his death in the spring of 1702, William had appointed Marlborough as Captain-General of the English army and Ambassador Extraordinary to the Dutch United Provinces.

Marlborough controlled an army whose last great Continental victory had been at Agincourt, 300 years earlier. He faced a French army undefeated in a major land engagement for six decades. However, his first campaign as commander, in 1702, was a great success: he cleared the River Meuse of French occupation, and returned to London to receive a dukedom and a £5,000 pension from Queen Anne.

1703 was more frustrating: Marlborough's Dutch allies refused to allow him to attack the French, even in the most promising of circumstances. Meanwhile he was dogged by

The general who never lost a battle: Sir Godfrey Kneller's portrait of the Duke of Marlborough

sniping from the Commons, whose Tory majority wanted a naval war rather than expensive troop deployments for the defence of the Dutch.

In 1704, eager to slip his Dutch controllers, and keen to save Vienna from imminent Franco-Bavarian assault, Marlborough led his army from the North Sea to the Danube in a 250-mile march. It was a model of efficient planning, of the type that earned him the appreciative nickname among his troops of 'Corporal John'. On 2 July the allies secured their foothold in Bavaria when they stormed the hill fort of the Schellenberg, which guarded Donauworth.

Marlborough pushed on, hoping that he and Prince Eugene of Savoy would be able to lure the Elector of Bavaria and Marshals Marsin and Tallard into battle. The Franco-Bavarians were astonished, on 13 August, to find their 60,000-strong army being attacked by a smaller allied force. Fatal mistakes saw the French coop up their men in the village of Blenheim, which gave its name to the battle. Eugene's fierce defence against superior numbers on the right flank, and Marlborough's deft touch, won a victory so huge that of the 4,500 French and Bavarian officers who fought that day, only 250 were not killed, wounded or taken prisoner.

Marlborough fought again at Ramillies in 1706. Here, subtle sleight of hand brought overwhelming triumph in less than two hours – and this despite the battleground having been selected by the enemy, long in advance. Two years later, at Oudenarde, Marlborough resumed his famous partnership with Prince Eugene, and again won handsomely, pushing the French from Flanders.

In 1709, at Malplaquet, the Duke encountered Villars, the greatest of Louis' latter-day soldiers. Villars understood Marlborough's battle plan: select a point in the enemy front and attack it hard; if that point gives way, then all well and good; if not, look for the section which had been weakened to reinforce the point of attack, and fire in your reserves there. In what was the bloodiest of all his battles, Marlborough won the field, but lost 18,000 men. The French suffered just 11,000 casualties.

In September 1711 Marlborough pierced the French defensive lines and took Bouchain. It was a brilliantly executed plan; and it was the swansong of his active career. The Tories, restored to power, started to broker peace. Marlborough was sidelined, and eventually replaced, his wife finally having burned her bridges with the Queen after years of tension. Voluntary exile followed on the Continent, where the Duke was still greeted as a hero. He was restored to many of his offices on the Hanoverian accession, but he was in his sixties by then, and his health was poor. The fierce migraines that had afflicted him throughout his life now gave way to debilitating strokes. He died in 1722.

In his final years he busied himself with plans for Blenheim Palace. It was a controversial project, of huge expense. However, it remains today a splendid memorial to one of Britain's greatest generals; indeed, there has never been a superior one. Perhaps only Cromwell, Wellington and Slim can claim parity.

Montgomery of Alamein
Nigel Hamilton

When the new Labour government began drawing up 'rewards' for the nation's heroes in the wake of World War II, it was decided to vote them not money but titles – which were cheaper. 'Bomber' Harris, commander-in-chief of the RAF's bomber squadrons that had firebombed Hamburg and Dresden, was famously denied a peerage, but viscountcies and earldoms were conferred like confetti by the leaders of the working classes.

If Field Marshal Sir Bernard Montgomery found this ironic, he did not object – indeed his staff espied him practising his preferred title for several weeks before the announcement was finally made in the New Year's Honours List, 1946. His grandfather, Sir Robert Montgomery, had been knighted for his work as Lieutenant-Governor of the Punjab, and his father, Bishop Henry Montgomery, had been awarded an honorary knighthood of the Order of St Michael and St George. Bernard Law Montgomery, as the third son and black sheep of the Bishop's family, was determined to best them, and this he finally did, as Field Marshal the Viscount Montgomery of Alamein, KG, GCB, DSO.

That profoundly competitive urge lay at the core of 'Monty', the 'little Field Marshal' – the most distinctive and successful British battlefield commander of the 20th century. With his black beret with two badges, he had become a household name across the globe in the autumn of 1942, rising out of complete obscurity to beat Field Marshal Rommel's Axis army at the Battle of Alamein in October of that year – a battle which marked the turning of the military tide against Hitler.

In the years after Monty's retirement, in 1958, it became almost *de rigueur* among military historians in Britain and America to belittle his achievement and to see his victories as inevitable triumphs of brute Allied force behind a mask of bombast and self-advertisement. This was unfortunate, because Montgomery was in many ways the most professional battlefield commander in British (and American) history.

Born in 1887 in the vicarage of St Mark's, Kennington, in South London, Bernard Law Montgomery spent his formative years in Tasmania, or Van Diemen's Land, where his father was made the island's first missionary bishop in 1889. He gained an early reputation for psychological maladjustment – being constantly caned by his mother for inappropriate behaviour and punished at school, and ultimately facing dismissal from the Royal Military Academy, Sandhurst, for grievous bodily harm against a fellow cadet.

Soldiering on the North-West Frontier of India as a subaltern, however, offered Montgomery a professional outlet for his aggressive nature, as well as responsibilities for his men's welfare that he relished. He won the DSO in hand-to-hand combat in Belgium in 1914 and, although wounded so severely that his grave was dug, he returned to the trenches of the Western Front in 1916 for the duration of World War I, participating as a staff officer in the bloodiest battles, from the suicidal battles of the Somme and Passchendaele to the infamous Chemin des Dames and, finally, the Allied counteroffensive that led to the Armistice of 11 November 1918. He ended the war as a decorated lieutenant-colonel and chief of staff of an entire division.

Montgomery had been appalled by the casualties (some 600,000 on the Allied side) incurred at the Battle of the Somme, in which his brigade was thrown into annihilating combat three times for the gain of a few hundred yards. As he wrote the next year to his brother, the Canadian soldiers were 'magnificent' at straightforward fighting, but they lacked 'soldierly instincts'. In Montgomery's view, 'the whole art of war' was now no longer glory but was 'to gain your objective with as little loss as possible'.

This was not a view held by the Commander-in-Chief of British and Commonwealth forces in France, Field Marshal Haig. 'Three years of war and the loss of one-tenth of the manhood of the nation is not too great a price to pay in so great a cause,' he had lectured newspaper correspondents before the Somme. Haig's reputation as a general would be dutifully protected after the war by patriotic British military historians who saw no alternative to the attritional bloodletting that characterised European hostilities in a modern industrialised era. For the professional soldiers who survived, however, there were but four choices: to resign from the army; to resign themselves to such warfare-by-numbers; to seek alternative weapons and methods of combat (such as armoured and air warfare); or to revolutionise the art of high command.

Monty chose the last. Field Marshal Haig became his object lesson in how *not* to command great armies in the field. In a real democracy men – professional soldiers, part-time soldiers ('Territorials'), as well as volunteers and conscripts in war – should be trained not as cannon fodder but as human beings capable of undertaking almost any reasonable task, provided that they were properly rehearsed in advance and informed of what was expected of them and that first-class planning was carried out. Unlike Haig, who was a dour, taciturn Scot incapable of public speaking, Monty had a crystal-clear mind, a sharp tongue, a sense of humour, irrepressible energy and an ebullient ego. As an ex-'colonial' from Tasmania he had a healthy contempt for the establishment, for social hierarchy, for ceremonial and for 'bellyaching' – the finding of reasons for not doing things. Where Haig had, in his forties, suddenly married an aristocratic lady-in-waiting to the Queen, Monty first proposed to a 17-year-old music student, then – when she turned him down – to a 39-year-old war widow, an artist with two children. Despite his essentially homosocial orientation, it proved an inspired choice, for Betty Carver not only bore Monty a son of his own, but provided a quality of companionship and affection he had simply never known in his childhood or adult years. Although he still sailed close to the wind on occasion, Betty helped him curb his insubordinate nature and ego until he was, in 1937, finally given command of a brigade, the stepping-stone to becoming a general.

Betty Carver's death in October 1937 was the turning point in Montgomery's personal life. He suffered a physical breakdown two years later, while commanding a division in

The full Monty: poster advertising an Army documentary on Montgomery's victory in North Africa

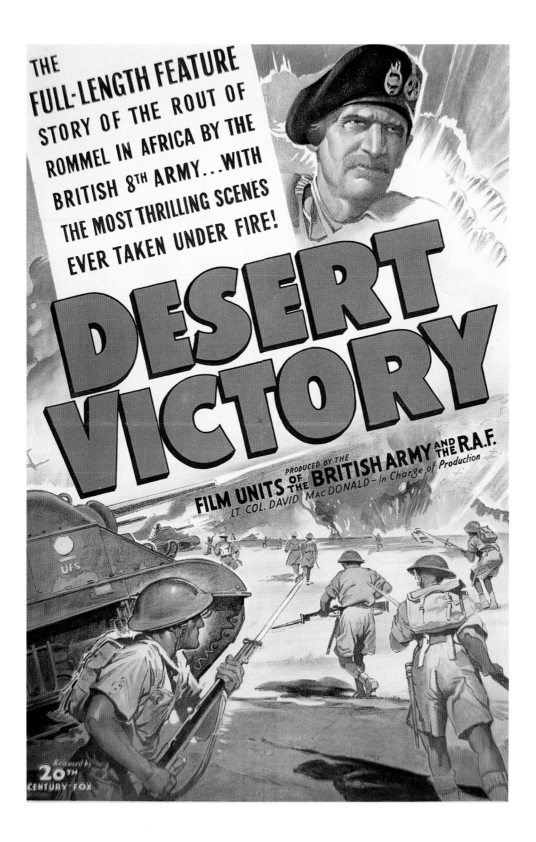

Palestine, but was determined to take a regular army division to France if war broke out. Eventually, after being put in a pool of unemployed officers in August 1939, he got his way, his men and an opportunity to show that a British army division, properly trained, was just as professional and effective as its German equivalent. Rehearsing his troops not in attack but in fighting retreat months *before* Hitler's invasion of the Low Countries and France, Monty's division became the backbone of the British Expeditionary Force as the French and Belgian armies crumbled and Hitler's Panzer forces swept behind the British lines to Boulogne and Calais. Monty brought back almost his entire division from the beaches of Bray-Dunes and Dunkirk, but his bitter denunciation of the incompetence of his Commander-in-Chief, General Lord Gort, earned him only rebuke and Winston Churchill's refusal to give him a battlefield command.

Only by accident was Montgomery ultimately given field command, following a seemingly endless series of British defeats stretching from Hong Kong, Singapore, Greece, Crete and Tobruk to the Egyptian village of Alamein, 60 miles from Cairo, in the summer of 1942. Monty's complete 'new broom' – sacking useless officers, visiting the frontline troops, laying down the plan of battle before it started, and rehearsing every aspect in advance with live ammunition and simulated signals – led to the sterling defensive battle of Alam Halfa at the end of August 1942, when Rommel's hopes of smashing through to Cairo with his Panzer divisions were irrevocably defeated, and the subsequent Battle of Alamein, starting on 24 October 1942 – a battle in which the Axis army in Egypt was destroyed, 30,000 of its men surrendering and the rest forced to retreat 1,500 miles into Tunisia, where they were finally killed or taken captive in May 1943.

Carrying out thereafter, with General George S. Patton, the vast amphibious invasion of Sicily, Montgomery demonstrated that an Allied army could never again be defeated by German forces, providing it was properly commanded and trained. Allied near-disasters at Salerno, near Naples, and later at Anzio, north of Rome, only proved his point. True generalship, Montgomery railed, was not simply the rugged acceptance of casualties, as in World War I, but the planning and rehearsal of one's forces to ensure the successful outcome of a battle before it even started.

At the insistence of the Deputy Prime Minister, Clement Attlee, Montgomery was, shortly before Christmas 1943, made Commander-in-Chief of four Allied armies – one British, one Canadian and two American – for the invasion of Normandy, scheduled to take place in the summer of 1944. Launched on 6 June 1944, the Allied D-Day landings, against an enemy-held coast defended by up to 59 German divisions, not only proved triumphantly successful, but led to the greatest German defeat ever suffered in a single battle in the west. As the Allied armies roared across the Seine and liberated Paris several days in advance of Montgomery's 90-day schedule in late August 1944, the victorious Battle of Normandy looked somehow inevitable. Allied Supreme Commander General Eisenhower, however, knew differently. The battle, in which the German armies in the west suffered nearly half a million casualties, had been a titanic struggle in itself – but getting the troops prepared, inspired and into battle in such a way that, despite storms and local setbacks, they could not be dislodged or defeated by the forces at Hitler's disposal was a miracle. It had been and would probably remain forever the greatest assault landing in human history. 'I don't know if we could have done it without Monty.' Eisenhower later confided. 'Whatever they say about him, he got us there' – and it was in recognition of this historic achievement that Winston Churchill, as Prime Minister, promoted Monty to field marshal.

Triumph was followed by tragedy at Arnhem (the 'Bridge Too Far') and a stop-go nightmare winter in which Montgomery was asked to take command of two reeling American armies in the Battle of the Bulge, then crossed the Rhine with three Allied armies under his command, only to be stopped by Eisenhower from taking Berlin, which was left to the Soviets. Shaking his head, Montgomery took the unconditional capitulation of all German forces in the north of Germany and Holland on 4 May 1945, signing his name with a simple twopenny pen under the canvas mess tent of his mobile tactical headquarters. Taking off his tortoiseshell glasses, he announced in front of whirring BBC cameras and microphones, 'And that concludes the surrender'.

Montgomery had shown, like Nelson, what true, dedicated and professional leadership can do in a democracy. He died on 24 March 1976 and is buried in a simple English churchyard, in Binstead, Surrey. His posthumous statue, by Oscar Nemon, stands sentinel in Whitehall, facing the gates of Downing Street – a reminder of the renascence of British military arms under his professional command in World War II, and of performances on the field of battle which had finally matched the rhetoric and inspiration of Winston Churchill.

Lord Nelson
Andrew Roberts

Admiral Lord Nelson is unquestionably Britain's greatest naval hero. His memory is still toasted every 21 October on the anniversary of his last and greatest victory, the battle of Trafalgar in 1805. His story is a sublime one of patriotism, courage and leadership: two centuries after his death it still has the power to thrill the hearts of Britons.

Born in Burnham Thorpe in Norfolk on 29 September 1758, the fifth surviving son of its rector Edmund Nelson, Horatio Nelson went to sea aged only 12, on the 64-gun warship *Raisonnable* under the command of his maternal uncle Captain Maurice Suckling. It is said that he was violently seasick. His first real sea-going experience was gained on a journey to the West Indies on a merchantman, and soon afterwards he rejoined his uncle on the harbour guardship *Triumph*.

Suckling ensured that the boy became skilled at navigation and boat-sailing, and Nelson soon had an expert knowledge of the pilotage of the Medway and the Thames. His training in practical seamanship could not have been better, and at the age of 14 he was chosen for an Arctic voyage, as coxswain of the captain's gig. On his return, he was sent to the East Indies on board the 20-gun *Seahorse*. Travelling to every station 'from Bengal to Bassorah', his health broke down and he was invalided home.

It was a depressing period for Nelson, but also one that seems to have fired him with a powerful sense of personal destiny. 'I almost wished myself overboard,' he later said of this time. 'But a sudden glow of patriotism was kindled within me. Well then, I exclaimed, I will be a hero, and confiding in Providence I will brave every danger.' By April 1777 Nelson was 18, had passed his naval examinations and had been promoted to second lieutenant aboard the 32-gun frigate *Lowestoft*, under the command of his great friend Captain William Locker.

Locker's military philosophy was simple: 'Lay a Frenchman close and you will beat him.' It was a lesson that Nelson was to take to heart. After serving with Locker in Jamaica, he was promoted to post-captain and then – only four months short of his 21st birthday – transferred to the flagship of the Commander-in-Chief, Sir Peter Parker. He rose by dint of his charm, intelligence, application and great maritime ability, but neither was he hindered by Suckling's promotion to the comptrollership of the Royal Navy. Nepotism might have been an 18th-century vice, but it certainly helped along the career of Britain's finest master and commander.

In January 1780, by then captaining a frigate, Nelson took part in the disastrous amphibious assault against the Spanish possessions of San Juan. Yellow fever killed the vast majority of the British seamen, and Nelson himself survived only because he was recalled to Jamaica, afterwards returning to England where he had to spend a year rebuilding his health.

England expects: Horatio Nelson as a young captain in 1781, painted by John Francis Rigaud

When he did go back to sea, sailing to Canada, he got 'knocked up with scurvy'. Nelson's was always a delicate constitution, which makes his achievements all the more remarkable.

It was while he was commanding the frigate HMS *Boreas*, on an unpopular mission to prevent Britain's West Indian colonists trading with the now independent United States of America, that Nelson married a young widow from the island of Nevis, Mrs Frances Nesbit. There followed six years of peace, in which Nelson had to eke out an existence on half-pay, living with his parents. On the outbreak of war with Revolutionary France in 1793, however, he was at last given his first large ship, the 64-gun frigate *Agamemnon*, and ordered to join the Mediterranean Fleet. It was when he was at Naples that he met his celebrated future mistress Emma Hamilton, the wife of the British minister there, Sir William Hamilton.

On 12 July 1794, while besieging the Corsican town of Calvi, a cannonball struck the ground near where Nelson was standing, the splinters blinding him in his right eye. The next year, after a daring and successful attack against the French outside Toulon, Admiral Sir John Jervis appointed Nelson to the rank of commodore.

Three years later, fighting under Jervis during the battle of Cape St Vincent, Nelson displayed his flair for independent decision-making. Risking court-martial and disgrace for leaving the line of battle, Nelson – having spotted that the two divided sections of the Spanish fleet were about to reunite – sailed his ship HMS *Captain* into the 80-gun *San Nicolas* and led a boarding party which captured her. No sooner had the Spanish vessel struck her colours than – shouting 'Westminster Abbey or glorious victory!' – Nelson proceeded to board an even larger enemy ship that had drifted alongside, the 112-gun *San Josef*. Jervis embraced Nelson when he went aboard the flagship after the battle; the commodore was knighted and promoted to rear-admiral.

Soon afterwards, leading an expedition to try to capture a Spanish treasure ship sheltering at Tenerife, Nelson lost his right arm to grapeshot from the fortress of Santa Cruz. 'A left-handed admiral will never again be considered,' he lamented. 'I am become a burden to my friends and useless to my country.'

Events the following year spectacularly proved otherwise. It was Nelson's inspired guess that General Bonaparte's fleet – which had slipped past the British blockade of Toulon – had made for Egypt, and on the evening of 1 August 1798 Nelson finally caught up with it at anchor in Aboukir Bay at the mouth of the Nile. By sailing round the head of the French line to attack from the landward side, Nelson won one of the most decisive victories in naval history. Only four French ships escaped out of seventeen, and Napoleon's army was left utterly stranded in Asia.

Nelson was elevated to the peerage and deluged with valuable presents from, among others, the Tsar of Russia, the Sultan of Turkey, the City of London and the East India Company. It was while he was recuperating in Naples from a severe wound to the forehead incurred during the battle of the Nile that he fell in love with Lady Hamilton. Although it has been presented by romantics as one of the great love affairs of history, in fact she seems to have been a rather irritating woman, who did nothing to prick Nelson's understandable tendency to vanity.

For all Nelson's genius at the Nile, nothing could be done by Britain to hinder Napoleon's domination of the European continent. In order to maintain the British blockade of France, for complex political reasons it sadly became necessary to attack the Danish fleet at Copenhagen in April 1801. Vice-Admiral Nelson was second-in-command to Admiral Parker, and when he was ordered to 'discontinue the action' he put his telescope to his blind eye and joked: 'I really do not see the signal.' The subsequent victory completely vindicated this act of gross insubordination.

At the end of Britain's short-lived Peace of Amiens with France, Nelson was appointed to command the Royal Navy in the Mediterranean, where he proceeded to blockade Toulon, not stepping off his flagship HMS *Victory* for more than ten days over the next two years. Meanwhile, with a vast army at Boulogne ready to cross the Channel at the first moment the Navy could be decoyed away, the newly crowned Emperor Napoleon posed by far the greatest invasion threat to the United Kingdom between the Spanish Armada in 1588 and the fall of France in 1940.

It was not to be until 21 October 1805 that Nelson managed to close with the enemy, after a long and exhausting transatlantic journey to the West Indies attempting to track down the large Franco-Spanish combined fleet under the command of the French Admiral Pierre Villeneuve. In essence, Nelson's battle plan at Trafalgar was to sail through the enemy's line in two columns, cutting it roughly into equal thirds, and then to concentrate the British firepower on the rear two-thirds, thus equalling up the numbers between the combined fleets' 33 ships and the British fleet's 27. It was imaginative and daring and was nicknamed by his captains 'the Nelson Touch'.

The plan was also superbly successful, although it required great skill and courage to implement it since the enemy were able to fire broadsides into the British ships for an agonisingly long time before they were in a position to respond. Nelson led one column in HMS *Victory*, Rear-Admiral Cuthbert Collingwood the other. It was just before battle was joined that Nelson ordered the hoisting of his famous and stirring signal to the fleet: 'England expects that every man will do his duty.'

Everything went precisely according to Nelson's specifications, except that during the battle a sniper up in the rigging of the French 74-gun *Redoubtable* shot Nelson himself, the ball striking his left shoulder and mortally wounding him. 'They have done for me at last,' he told *Victory*'s Captain Hardy. 'My backbone is shot through.' Before Nelson died, however, Hardy was able to inform him that 14 enemy ships had surrendered, for the loss of not one single British vessel. 'Thank God I have done my duty,' answered Nelson, as he slipped into immortal glory.

Overleaf: *The end of Napoleon's plans to invade Britain: the Battle of Trafalgar*

Florence Nightingale
Julian Spilsbury

'We are ducks who have hatched a wild swan!'

Fanny Nightingale wasn't being fair to herself or her family. The Nightingales were well-bred and well-connected, counting the Palmerstons and Sidney Herbert, heir presumptive to the Earl of Pembroke, among their circle of friends. Fanny's husband William Nightingale was wealthy, and she had had the highest social ambitions for their two daughters. The second of these – their 'swan' – had been given the outlandish name of Florence, after the city of her birth. (It could have been worse: her older sister had been born in Naples and named Parthenope after that city's Greek name.) If 'Parthe' was a problem – subject to nerves and devoted to the point of mania to her younger sister – Florence was, if anything, even more of a worry. Witty, attractive, blessed – or cursed – with the gift of inspiring 'passions' in women and men, Florence was also strange, troubled, withdrawn. At 16, she later recalled, 'God spoke to me and called me to his service'. Her private writings from then on contain all the turmoil – the agonies, ecstasies, self-disgust and sense of personal unworthiness – of a 17th-century Puritan diary. As with the Puritans, her call when it came was a call to action; but in what sphere?

If Florence had told her family she wanted to dance in the music halls they could not have been more horrified. Nursing was not a respectable profession for a well-bred young lady in Protestant societies – that it was so in Catholic countries did not help. Nurses, of whom Dickens' Mrs Gamp was the archetype, were regarded as drunkards and prostitutes; some, indeed, were both. There followed 14 years of struggle with her family, involving tantrums, tears, reconciliations and the near-commitment of 'poor Parthe', before Florence was able to escape the gilded pointlessness of a Victorian lady's life and, without Fanny or Parthe's blessing, begin her life's work, at a London home for distressed gentlewomen. By then, with her lifelong passion for lists and her voracious appetite for hard work, she was already an acknowledged expert in her field. Soon, though, she was champing at the bit, searching for a wider sphere of action. In 1853 the Eastern Question provided it.

It is often forgotten that the Crimean War was regarded at the time as a just and popular one. Redcoats marched to the docks through cheering crowds, who later thrilled to the reports of their bloody victory at the Alma. After the pride came the fall; William Howard Russell's despatches to *The Times* revealed to a shocked nation the appalling state of the army's administrative and medical arrangements. Thanks to years of official neglect, the troops arrived in the Crimea without any kind of hospital transport. The wounded and sick – cholera had decimated the army before the first shot was fired – were carried down to the beaches by comrades, bandsmen and sailors, or by the French, to be ferried across the Black Sea to the barrack hospital at Scutari. The commissariat was tightly bound in red tape – a Byzantine system of warrants and requisitions without which nothing could be issued. The men who ran the system, the commissaries and purveyors, were a second eleven of timid souls, who lived on their salaries, were desperate for promotion, and were dependent for both on the army's Chief Medical Officer, Dr John Hall, a man who impressed even Lord Cardigan with his ability to terrify subordinates. Hall it was who had been sent by Lord Raglan to inspect the hospital at Scutari and had reported that it 'has now been put on a very creditable footing … nothing is lacking'.

Apart, that is, from bedding, furniture, operating tables, screens, soap, towels, hospital clothing, boilers, kettles, utensils, rations suitable for the sick, drugs, chamber pots, a functioning laundry, adequate kitchens, fuel, an untainted water supply – anything, in short, which could make the building habitable even by healthy men. Worst of all – and as yet undiscovered – defective sanitation made the hospital a deathtrap. The nation was quick to respond: from public subscriptions *The Times* raised an unprecedented £30,000. Sidney Herbert, now Minister at War, wrote to Florence asking her to go out at once with 40 handpicked nurses; his letter crossed with hers offering her services.

Arriving in early November 1854, Florence and her 'ladies' were welcomed by the military authorities through gritted teeth, patronised and sidelined. Appalled by what they saw, many of her nurses wanted to set to at once, but Florence kept them sorting linen and deferred at all points to the powers-that-were. She was not going to commit her forces piecemeal, where they would alleviate just enough suffering to allow the system to stagger on. Only catastrophe, she knew, would give her the absolute power she needed; if in the meantime individuals went on suffering, so be it. There was a steeliness, even ruthlessness, in Florence's character that shocked those who encountered it. Her passion, all-consuming, was for humanity as a whole. Closer intimacies were not encouraged.

The awaited catastrophe was not long in coming. Casualties from the battle of Inkerman, and the terrible Crimean winter, came flooding in. It is difficult to exaggerate the horrors of that time, with rows of amputees lying in their own and others' filth, so pitifully embarrassed at their condition that they begged the nurses not to come near them. The system collapsed – and the authorities turned in desperation to Miss Nightingale.

A German general once remarked that any reasonably competent officer could command a division, but that it took a genius to supply one. Florence was such a genius. Armed with sole discretion in the spending of *The Times'* £30,000, 'unlimited power of drawing on the government', and the ear of her old friend (and the platonic love of her life) Sidney Herbert, she became, in effect, purveyor to the hospital and soon, in fact and nickname, 'Lady-in-Chief'. Out of the money at her disposal she provided every single necessity for the hospital, from socks and nightcaps to medical equipment – doctors soon learned to bypass official channels and come straight to her for all their needs. She organised the kitchens with new boilers and oversaw the cooking; she bought 200 scrubbing brushes and saw to the scrubbing of the wards and corridors; she hired Turkish laundresses and

Overleaf: The Mission of Mercy: Florence Nightingale Receiving the Wounded at Scutari *by Jerry Barrett, 1857*

supervised their work; she provided a regiment that had come out in tropical kit with warm clothing procured in Constantinople. She started a soldiers' 'dry' canteen, a reading room, four schools, a remittance scheme whereby men could send money home. She worked 20 hours a day, every day; and last thing at night – the start, this, of the legend – she paced the corridors lamp in hand and simply talked to the men.

Of course there was a reaction. A military man as well as a doctor, Hall knew the value of a well-timed counterattack. Newly armed with a KCB – Florence dubbed it 'Knight of the Crimean Burial-grounds' – Hall set out to put the upstart in her place. To his policy of obstruction and petty persecutions he added a whispering campaign, fuelled sectarian wranglings between Catholic and Protestant nurses, and encouraged those nurses who chafed under Florence's iron discipline.

Help came from an unexpected quarter – a woman her own age, whose own early adulthood had been a constant battle against her family. An unlikely quarter too, for Queen Victoria was no champion of women's rights, other than her own. Yet, in a letter to Sidney Herbert, the Queen wrote:

> Let Mrs Herbert … know that I wish Miss Nightingale and the ladies would tell these poor noble wounded and sick men that no-one takes a warmer interest or feels more for their sufferings or admires their courage and heroism more than their Queen. Day and night she thinks of her beloved troops. So does the Prince. Beg Mrs Herbert to communicate these words to those ladies, as I know our sympathy is valued by those noble fellows.

The letter was read out in the hospital wards and, propped in their cots, men who had stormed the Great Redoubt or charged through the guns at Balaclava listened with tears in their eyes. If the senior officers grumbled, they did so in secret; Florence had outflanked them yet again. As for the soldiers, in the batteries above Sevastopol they cheered her three times three and strewed her way with flowers.

Florence came home a national heroine, yet bereaved, dogged with a sense of failure. 'Oh my poor men…' she wrote in her private notes, 'I am a bad mother to come home and leave you in your Crimean graves.' And again and again, on margins, in every available space: 'I can never forget … I can never forget.' These terrible words drove her on for the rest of her life. By the time she died in 1910, the first female holder of the Order of Merit – she declined a place in Westminster Abbey and was carried to her family grave by six sergeants – she had founded training schools for nurses, advanced the cause of public health and sanitation at home and worldwide, and transformed the theory and practice of military medicine.

More, perhaps, even than that, Florence Nightingale changed forever the nation's perception of two professions – the one she came to personify, and the one of which she was the unfailing champion. She found them neglected, despised. She left them so firmly rooted in the national consciousness that to this day politicians jostle to bask in their reflected glory – the nurse and the soldier.

The Old Contemptibles
Max Arthur

By the middle of August 1914 train stations all over Britain were echoing to the tramp of newly studded boots and the clattering of Lee Enfield rifles as thousands of soldiers of the British Expeditionary Force prepared for their first military engagement in Western Europe since the Battle of Waterloo in 1815. Their task was to stop the ruthless German army, which had marched through neutral Belgium anticipating that they would be swilling champagne or absinthe in Paris by September.

Kaiser Wilhelm II, with great faith in his army's ability to execute Count von Schlieffen's plan and sweep across northern Europe, regarded the BEF as little more than an irritant to be removed, along with the French and the Belgians. Two weeks after war had been declared, and with the bulk of the BEF in place in the Mons area, the Kaiser issued an order of the day from his headquarters in Aix-la-Chapelle: 'It is my royal and imperial command that you concentrate your energies for the immediate present upon one simple purpose, and that is that you address all your skills and all the valour of my soldiers to exterminate first the treacherous English; walk over General French's contemptible little army.'

It is seldom wise to insult your enemy, especially a bunch of British Tommies, for not only does it make them gird their loins, it increases their sense of defiance and a strong desire to put their bayonet where it hurts most. They adopted the slur as a badge of pride and were soon widely known as the 'Old Contemptibles'. The Kaiser, who had attended army manoeuvres in England in 1909, accompanied by Winston Churchill, had totally failed to understand the British soldier, or to recognise that rehearsals are not the real thing.

Having declared war on 4 August 1914, four infantry divisions and one cavalry division of the BEF began embarking under conditions of great secrecy on 6 August, and ten days later, spectacularly, the bulk of the force had arrived in France without a single casualty. So successful were the arrangements to maintain secrecy that regiments left their barracks without being told where they were going, and entered trains where the drivers had to wait for last-minute instructions. Everyone knew, of course, that they were heading for France, but not at which port they would land. There are parallels here with what happened 30 years later on the beaches of Normandy.

The two harbours chosen were Le Havre and Boulogne. The first sight for the welcoming Boulonnais was the Argyll and Sutherland Highlanders, resplendent in their kilts, with a fine show of bare knees as they marched like liberators to the swirl of bagpipes. The women adored them and covered them in kisses and flowers.

The Scots' main task was to prepare the campsite for the thousands of troops who were to follow. In those hectic days transatlantic liners and other smaller ships unloaded not only

Overleaf: *Privates Raper, Crockett and Beckham of the British Expeditionary Force*

the troops but massive supplies. Most of the men were between 25 and 35, many of them reservists, and there was a fair sprinkling of Boer War ribbons. This was a superbly fit and highly trained and motivated army, proud of its regimental and corps traditions – an army of artillerymen, sappers, dragoons, hussars, lancers and, of course, the backbone of the BEF, the infantrymen. These infantrymen were capable of the extraordinary rate of fire of 15 rounds per minute. Not an army to be underestimated.

The BEF had not only 'God on their side' but a message from their king: 'You are leaving home to fight for the safety and honour of my Empire … I have implicit confidence in you, my soldiers.' They also carried in their paybooks a letter from Field Marshal Kitchener, whose pointing finger was later to exhort many a doubtful young man into a change of heart and to join up. In it he states: 'You are ordered abroad as a soldier of the King, to help our French comrades against the invasion of a common enemy.' Ever the moraliser, he then adds, sanctimoniously: 'You may find temptations both in wine and women. You must entirely resist both temptations and while treating all women with perfect courtesy, you should avoid any intimacy. Do your duty. Fear God. Honour the King.' With lines like that it was little wonder the brothels of both ports were lined with queues of Tommies.

Although a confident army, the BEF was still a small one compared with those of its European neighbours. It was an army used to policing the British Empire, not prepared for fighting large-scale wars. Britain's real strength lay in the might of the Royal Navy, and in those sunlit Edwardian days no one thought King George would move 90,000 men to fight his cousin Wilhelm, who 13 years earlier had been at their grandmother Queen Victoria's deathbed.

The BEF were the first to draw blood when, just after dawn on 22 August 1914, C Squadron of the 4th Irish Dragoon Guards sent out patrols north of Soignies, and on the road leading from Maisières spotted cavalrymen of the 2nd Kuirassiers. Corporal Thomas opened fire, the first British soldier to do so in what was to become known as the Great War. His troop commander led his men in pursuit of the enemy. With some pride, he returned to his commanding officer and presented his sword covered in German blood. The Royal Army Medical Corps noted that they stitched up three wounded enemy, all of whom had suffered sword cuts. Little, it seemed, had changed in warfare in the 99 years since Waterloo.

The British newspapers the following day proclaimed that the British troops had drawn first blood, and that their opening attack had been totally successful.

The Old Contemptibles first confronted the enemy *en masse* at Mons on 23 August, and held their position, inflicting severe casualties on the Germans and arresting their lightning advance. The 4th Division arrived from England to take part in the savage fighting three days later, after the British had withdrawn to Le Cateau. From here the BEF withdrew in a fighting retreat to St Quentin in good spirits, the Germans being too exhausted by their losses to pursue in any great force. The BEF were reinforced by the 6th Division for their advance to the Aisne. The 7th Division, made up of highly trained soldiers from throughout the Empire, provided further reinforcements, but by the end of the First Battle of Ypres the BEF's casualties were severe.

As each side manoeuvred to outflank the other, the front expanded. Weary troops simply dug in for protection, and within a few months the front stretched from the Swiss border to the northern coast. In November the ever-impatient Kaiser, eager for some success, ordered his Imperial Foot Guards into the attack. They attacked at Ypres in close-order formation, with the loss of thousands of men and absolutely no gain at all.

At the end of the First Battle of Ypres in November 1914 the winter weather brought intense cold, and both the British and the Germans sought the refuge of their trenches. With Christmas, the thoughts of soldiers on both sides turned to home. And it was from the yearning to be at home that a remarkable peace occurred throughout the trenches on the Western Front.

I interviewed the last survivor of the Old Contemptibles, Frank Sumpter, shortly before he died, aged 106. He proudly wore his 1914 Star with oak leaf attachment, which indicated that he had served throughout the campaign that ended with the Battle of Ypres in November 1914. He was the last man alive entitled to wear it. He was to recall of that unique Christmas truce: 'We could barely reach each other because the barbed wire was not just one fence; it was two or three fences together, with a wire in between. And so we just shook hands and I had the experience of talking to one German who said to me, "Do you know where the Essex Road in London is?" I replied, "Yes, my uncle had a shoe repairing shop there". He said, "That's funny. There's a barber shop on the other side where I used to work."

'They could all speak very good English because before the war Britain was invaded by Germans. Every pork butcher was German, every barber's shop was German, and they were all over here getting the low-down on the country. It's ironic, when you think about it, that he must have shaved my uncle so many times, and yet my bullet might have found him and his bullet might have found me.

'There were no shots fired, and some people enjoyed the curiosity of walking about in no-man's-land. It was good to walk around. Later, as a sign of their friendliness, the Germans put up a sign saying "Gott mit uns", which means, "God is with us". And so we put up a sign in English saying, "We got mittens too". I don't know if they enjoyed that joke.'

Frank Sumpter's story personifies the qualities of the Old Contemptibles. When, 90 years ago, the Kaiser ridiculed them he may have given them the name by which they have become known to history. But he had missed the essence of the British soldier: his sheer bloody doggedness, his sense of irony and his wicked black humour.

The Redcoat
Gary Sheffield

Scene 1: Waterloo, 18 June 1815. The Duke of Wellington orders his army to advance. The lines of redcoated British infantry, having repelled everything the French could throw at them all day, surge forward to complete the victory over Napoleon.

Scene 2: The St Lawrence River, Quebec, 13 September 1757. In the early hours British troops move stealthily along the river by barge. Scrambling up a steep cliff, the army of General James Wolfe forms up on the Plains of Abraham, having outflanked the French defences. The subsequent battle will break French power in North America and hand Canada to the British.

Scene 3: Gandamak, Afghanistan, 13 January 1842. A handful of men of the 44th Foot, the last remnants of a large column that retreated from Kabul a few days earlier, form a square as Afghan tribesmen move in for the kill. Fighting with the courage of desperation, the 44th are overwhelmed.

In defence and attack, in victory and defeat, the Redcoats made their mark on history. The British Army was a principal instrument by which a small island came to possess a global empire and emerge as a great power in Europe. Before the Battle of Waterloo Wellington pointed to an ordinary soldier and said, 'it depends all upon that article whether we do the business or not'. Wellington was, as usual, correct: 'that article' was a formidable practitioner of the business of war.

The term 'Redcoat' is synonymous with the British soldier from the mid-17th century to the late Victorian period, an era that embraces great European struggles such the Crimean War (1853–5) and the Revolutionary and Napoleonic Wars (1793–1815), as well as the gaining of an empire. Cromwell's New Model Army adopted the red jacket in 1644, at a time when armies across Europe were standardising their uniforms. The introduction of modern weapons in the mid-19th century made the wearing of bright colours impracticable on the battlefield – soldiers became easy targets – so it was progressively replaced by khaki (from the Urdu word for dust), at least on campaign. The red coat was last worn in action as late as 1885, in the Sudan.

Not all British soldiers wore the red coat. The Royal Artillery and some of the cavalry wore blue, while Rifle regiments wore green. Nor did Tommy Atkins (the traditional name for the British soldier) fight alone. At Waterloo, Wellington's Allied army contained Dutch-Belgian soldiers, as well as men from a variety of German states. Wellington's British troops

---

Redcoats advancing into battle at Waterloo, 1815, painted by R. Caton Woodville

were actually in a minority; and the battle was fought in conjunction with the Prussians. This – the British fighting alongside allies – has been the typical pattern for European wars. In the struggle for empire the British used large numbers of 'native' troops, from India, Africa and North America. Indeed, during the Indian Mutiny of 1857–8 the continued loyalty of Sikh and Gurkha troops was a vital factor in the British victory. Neither should we forget the Royal Navy, who made it possible for the Redcoats to get to foreign fields, and helped keep them in supply once they arrived. Often parties of sailors fought on land alongside the soldiers, the service of the Naval Brigade at the battle of Tel-el-Kebir in Egypt (1882) being a case in point.

So who were the Redcoats? They were all technically volunteers who had taken the king's shilling, not conscripts. Wellington notoriously described them as 'the scum of the earth', and indeed many enlisted to escape from poverty, because they had got a girl pregnant, or from some other ignoble motive. Some were more or less kidnapped and forced to enlist. Others, though, joined for adventure, or to better themselves, and the Iron Duke also commented on the fact that the Army turned the rank and file into 'fine fellows'. Life in the Army was tough, but for some it was an improvement on their civilian lot. For all that, for many working-class families a son joining the Army was a disgrace. When young William Robertson – the first man to rise, in the words of his memoirs, 'From Private to Field Marshal' – enlisted in 1877 his mother wrote, 'I'd rather Bury you than see you in a red coat'. Working-class antipathy was heightened by the fact that, in the years before the introduction of police forces, troops were often used to keep order and were, then as now, available to the government to break strikes. The so-called 'Peterloo Massacre' of 1819 in Manchester was the most notorious use of troops for domestic repression.

The 'conscription of hunger' worked particularly in the case of Ireland. In 1830 42 per cent of the rank and file were Irish, as opposed to 43.5 per cent English, although by the 1870s the respective figures were around 24 per cent and 59 per cent. For much of the Redcoat period men enlisted in the Army for what amounted to life. Short service was introduced in 1870, with men serving a number of years with the colours before going onto the reserve. Men sent overseas would not see Britain for years at a time. While a favoured few ended up as Chelsea Pensioners in the Royal Hospital, many soldiers' only reward was poverty on their discharge in Britain, or an early grave in a distant land.

Discipline was harsh. Until 1881 bad conduct was punished by flogging. Wellington's provost marshal restored order at the storming of Badajoz in 1812 by hanging soldiers caught in the act of looting. During the American War of Independence (1776–83) the rebels derided the British troops as 'bloody backs'. However, it would be wrong to see the Army as held together primarily by fear of the lash. Although the officers were drawn from the upper echelons of society, and there was a vast gulf between them and the men, they could share loyalty to the regiment and admire each other for soldierly qualities. The partnership between the NCOs and the officers was the motor that kept the regiment going. Some officers were noted for their enlightened attitudes towards their men, such as Sir John

Moore, the founding father of British light infantry, who was killed at the Battle of Corunna in 1809. As the 19th century wore on, paternalistic officers introduced a number of reforms.

Before about 1700 England/Great Britain was a fairly minor player in European affairs. The victories of the Duke of Marlborough helped launch Britain onto the world stage, and the Redcoat began to acquire his reputation as a formidable fighting man. From 1688 to 1815 Britain was at war with the French, the years without fighting amounting to truces rather than true peace. The Redcoat played a major role in a series of victories: Blenheim (1704), Minden (1757) and Salamanca (1812) among them. Even the American War of Independence was lost through a failure of seapower rather then defeat on land. In the wars of Empire, although not every battle was a victory – at Isandlwana (1879) a Zulu army destroyed a British force, and the Sikhs and Maoris proved to be formidable opponents – the British Army was highly effective. Today, the whole concept of imperialism is deeply unfashionable, and it would be dishonest to deny the dark side of Empire. It would be equally wrong, though, to decry the achievements of the British soldier, and his comrades-in-arms drawn from many races, in conquering, colonising and sustaining an enormous empire. The non-military legacy of the Redcoats was significant in many places. For example, Colonel John By founded a military outpost in Canada and built a canal to allow troops rapidly to be moved to the area. Renamed Ottawa, this settlement is now the Canadian capital.

The Redcoats' performance on the battlefield was undoubtedly impressive. In the hands of great generals like Marlborough, Wellington, Sir Garnett Wolseley or Lord Roberts they were world-beaters. In the hands of the less competent or the downright dim, as with Elphinstone on the retreat from Kabul in 1842 or Chelmsford during the 1879 Zulu War, their efficiency suffered. Yet in virtually all circumstances they demonstrated stoicism and endurance.

These qualities were epitomised by two of the Redcoats' characteristic tactics: the square and the so-called 'thin red line'. The square was a tight-knit formation with no open flanks, in which infantrymen would present bristling lines of bayonets that no horse would approach. It also proved very effective in colonial wars: at the battle of Ulundi (1879) a British square delivered devastating fire against attacking Zulus. The journalist William Howard Russell described the stand of the 93rd Highlanders at Balaclava in 1854 as the 'thin red streak tipped with a line of steel', which became corrupted into the more familiar 'thin red line'. British infantry was noted for its fire discipline, the ability of soldiers to hold their nerve in the face of attack and do maximum damage to the enemy at close range. Under Wellington, the two-deep British infantry line was often faced with dense columns of French attackers, but Napoleon's men rarely prevailed.

The Redcoat army is long gone. If few today know or care much about the Redcoats' campaigns, or their qualities of discipline, endurance and courage, then we are the poorer for it.

THE BLACK WATCH

The regimental system
Gary Sheffield

Visitors to the Joint Services Command and Staff College at Shrivenham are often struck by the appearance of the students. Those from the Royal Air Force are dressed pretty much alike, in light blue. The Royal Naval students have a similar appearance of uniformity, being clothed in dark blue and white. A glance at any group of British Army officers tells a very different story. They display a bewildering variety of military costume. Fusiliers wear a red and white feather hackle, disrespectfully known to other regiments as a dead parrot. Highland officers wear the kilt. The Royal Green Jackets are known, apparently illogically, as the 'Black Mafia', the sobriquet coming from the colour of their buttons. The Cheshire Regiment wears reddish-brown pullovers, while those of the Royal Artillery are blue. The King's Royal Hussars wear splendid crimson trousers, inherited from the 11th Hussars, the 'Cherrypickers'. An RAF officer once told me that on visits to the old Army Staff College at Camberley he used to play a game with a fellow airman. If they spotted two Army officers dressed identically they would shout 'snap'. He did this once, only for the soldier to pull up his trouser leg to reveal distinctly non-regulation socks.

The sheer diversity of uniform worn by British soldiers gives a clue as to the nature of the organisation. In a very real sense there is no such thing as 'the British Army'; rather, it is a loose federation of regiments and corps. Fiercely tribal, the British Army (I'll continue to use the term for convenience) isn't quite unique – some Commonwealth armies, such as the Canadians, have inherited the traditions – but it is a very different organisation from, say, the US Army, or indeed the RAF or Royal Navy. The British regimental system means that the soldier's primary allegiance is to a small unit, while the airman's or sailor's is to the larger organisation. While the latter are posted to a particular ship or squadron, and build up *esprit de corps* while they are there, they know that they will be posted to many other ships and squadrons in the course of their career. By contrast, it is unusual for an infantryman or Royal Armoured Corps soldier to move from regiment to regiment. Not every part of the British Army sticks to this format. Some of the larger corps such as the Royal Engineers and Royal Corps of Signals, as well as the Royal Artillery, which is technically a regiment, consist of a large number of smaller units, but their loyalty is to the corps. But for the infantry regiments, many of which have only one regular battalion, or the cavalry, which consists of single units, things are very different.

The current regimental system, as with so many other supposedly ancient traditions, is a creation of the Victorians, who imposed some order and logic on an older organisation. The British Army officially dates from 1661, a few months after the Restoration of King Charles II. Initially, regiments were known by the names of their colonels. There are still some

The badge and colours of The Black Watch (The 42nd Royal Highlanders)

survivals of those far-off days. In the early 18th century two regiments were commanded by colonels called Howard. As a way of telling them apart they were referred to by the colour of their facings (i.e. collar and cuffs); hence the Green Howards, a name borne by the regiment to this day.

Eventually, regiments were given numbers. One, raised in 1689, became the 22nd Regiment of Foot in the 18th century. In 1782 infantry regiments were given secondary territorial affiliations, and the 22nd acquired the title of Cheshire Regiment – appropriately enough, as the regiment had originally been recruited from the Chester area. The modern regiment styles itself the 22nd (Cheshire) Regiment, a reference to the fact that, highly unusually, it has never been amalgamated.

In many cases the 1782 affiliation of numbered regiments of foot to a county was fairly nominal. The Victorians changed all that. Edward Cardwell, who served in the 1870s as secretary of state for war, set in train a series of reforms that led in 1881 to the modern regimental system. Numbered infantry regiments (already since 1872 linked in pairs, one serving at home, the other overseas) were given county titles and affiliations, and local depots. In some cases, this was a natural and relatively painless process. The 43rd (Monmouthshire) and 52nd (Oxfordshire) Light Infantry had served together over many years, famously as part of Wellington's Light Division in the Napoleonic Wars, and were brought together as the Oxfordshire Light Infantry. In spite of the loss of the 43rd's title, the amalgamation was a happy one. The title 'Buckinghamshire' was added in 1908, to produce the name of the 'Ox & Bucks', as they were known throughout the Army – although the name was disliked by the regiment itself, which continued to refer to its battalions as the 43rd and 52nd. Even today, 40 years after a further amalgamation into the Royal Green Jackets, regimental old comrades will be introduced to the visitor as 'a 43rd' or '52nd' man!

In other cases the county affiliation was an example of the creation of an instant tradition. In 1881 the 14th Foot became the West Yorkshire Regiment, even though in 1782 it had been affiliated to Bedfordshire and in 1809 had swapped titles with the 16th Foot to become 'Buckinghamshire'. An even more extreme example was the Royal Sussex Regiment. Whereas the 1st Battalion had been the 35th Royal Sussex Regiment of Foot, the 2nd Battalion's previous incarnation had been the 107th Foot (Bengal Light Infantry) – a regiment raised from Europeans living in India.

Like another Victorian invention, the Dickensian Christmas, the county regimental system soon became so familiar that it was difficult to conceive of a time when it had not been there. It played to local pride and civic patriotism, a factor reinforced by the linking of part-time Volunteer (from 1908, Territorial) units into the county system. The county regiment was, and is, defined by a series of tribal totems. Usually it has a royal patron, which is reflected in the regimental title – say, The Argyll and Sutherland Highlanders (Princess Louise's). It has its own regimental march, cap badge and traditions. The colours, the flags originally carried into battle, are inscribed with honours awarded for long-ago actions. These are often commemorated with a special parade, followed by sports matches and some serious drinking. Some other regiments are traditionally friends and allies; others, deadly rivals.

The county regiment was the bedrock of the British Army in the two world wars. Even today, after a flurry of amalgamations and the occasional disbandment, the county regiment retains its importance. It has proved to be a very flexible organisation, capable of evolving without losing its original essence. The current Princess of Wales's Royal Regiment (PWRR), created in 1992, is the successor of most of the old infantry regiments of the south-east of England, its lineage including no less than 12 numbered regiments of foot. The PWRR has absorbed the traditions and ethos of its predecessors wonderfully well. This is reflected in the regimental badges: one worn on the sleeve depicts a royal tiger, passed down from the Royal Hampshires, while the cap badge includes a dragon (from the Buffs), ostrich plumes (from the Middlesex) and the Garter (from the Royal Sussex).

Much the same could be said of other 'large' infantry regiments created over the last four decades, such as the Light Infantry and the Royal Anglians. Similarly, there has been progressive amalgamation of cavalry regiments. The Light Dragoons was formed in 1992 from the 13th/18th and 15th/19th Hussars. Both parent regiments were themselves the result of amalgamations in 1922. In short, the regimental system is like a favourite old car kept going by constant attention. So many parts have been replaced with new ones, or with bits cannibalised from another vehicle, that little of the original remains: yet it is, to those who love it, still the same car.

Ruthless logic suggests that the regimental system is an anachronism that should be abolished. It builds inflexibility into the system – it would be much easier administratively if soldiers were 'trickle-posted' from unit to unit. The fierce tribalism makes it difficult to disseminate Army-wide doctrine. It is difficult to recruit in some areas (such as places with full employment), meaning that some regiments struggle to keep up to strength. In today's high intensity warfare, the Army often fights in mixed battlegroups of infantry and armour. This has led to suggestions such as that, while the title of, say, the Royal Scots Dragoon Guards might be maintained, it should cover a larger force of all arms rather than just tanks.

But the counter-argument is even stronger. The regimental system has proved to be remarkably flexible over the years; it is an excellent method of building high morale; and, above all, it works. If history teaches us anything, it is never to say never. For all that, it would take a very brave politician indeed to attempt to abolish the regimental system which has served the British Army so well for so long.

Robert the Bruce
Mick Imlah

Like most medieval heroes, the figure of Robert the Bruce, whose exploits were recorded in poems and chronicles composed a century after his death, is an alloy of historical fact and fairy tale. Yet the facts themselves are romantic enough. From being hounded as an outlaw to the wildest margins of his defeated country, he rose to become her undisputed king; and furthermore, by his own prowess and relentless will, secured her lasting freedom from a rich and overbearing island neighbour. Not much wonder that Scots, who owe their separate identity to the day of Bruce's making, still exhort one another in mock-heroic contexts to 'Remember Bannockburn!'.

For all that, the Bruce family has its origins in Normandy: the first 'Robert de Brus' took up lands in Yorkshire and Annandale in the 12th century as a reward for his hatred of the French. Good marriages consolidated the Bruces' rise in Scotland; not least, the union in 1271 of Robert, sixth Lord of Annandale, and the widow Marjory, Countess of Carrick. The first of their five sons, also called Robert, was born three years later at Turnberry Castle, at a time when the Scottish succession was about to stumble into crisis.

In 1286 and 1290 the successive deaths of King Alexander III and his infant heir Margaret terminated a brief period of stability in Scottish affairs, and King Edward I of England, an inveterate hater of Scots, muscled into the vacuum. He awarded the crown to John Balliol, agent of Scotland's foremost family the Comyns, over the rival claim of Robert Bruce the Elder, and at once began to boss and bully his nominee. Balliol eventually balked at Edward's treatment and raised an army of resistance; but his forces capitulated feebly at Dunbar (1296), while Edward's blitzed through the whole of Scotland in a matter of weeks.

With Balliol degraded and the Stone of Scone, traditionally the seat of Scottish kings, removed to Westminster, the burden of resistance was defiantly taken up by Sir William Wallace. The young Bruce, meanwhile, bided his time and minded his own interest: now declaring for the English king, now intriguing with dissenters – whichever seemed likeliest to damage the Comyns and advance his own claim. But when, in 1305, Wallace was betrayed and butchered, the perception that Bruce had scarcely opposed the rebel cause saw him dropped from favour in the settlement that followed.

Suddenly faced with suspicion or hostility on all sides, Bruce grew ragged in the assertion of his hopes. At an arranged meeting with John Comyn of Badenoch in February 1306, on the sacred ground of Grey Friars Church in Dumfries, he drew a knife and stabbed his rival. Six weeks after this outrage he was – in a manner of speaking – king; but his coronation was a rogue stratagem, an outlaw's declaration of civil war. He was reviled by the Scottish establishment and banished by the Church, and his foes began at once to hunt him down.

The patriot king: Robert the Bruce and his first wife

K: Robert Bruce begani his Raigne ⟨7⟩
1306

Robert dehis toye
Earle of Marr

The Earl of Pembroke surprised him with a night attack at Methven near Perth; and the self-styled Robert I found himself hiding in the forests of Argyll while his queen was imprisoned and three of his brothers put to death. According to the chronicler John of Fordun, he was obliged to spend the winter of 1306–7 alone on the little island of Rathlin off Antrim (though one of the larger Western Isles seems a likelier refuge), living off herbs and water and 'slighted by his servants'. Yet in the privations of this winter the legend of Robert the Bruce begins to take shape, in the form of stories, true or symbolical, of resolute spiders and hair's-breadth escapes. And now that national and personal survival were inseparable, the fortunes of Robert the Bruce and Scotland began to climb together out of the pit.

In the spring of 1307 Bruce was back in his own earldom of Carrick, where he got the better of two skirmishes with the occupying army, at Glen Trool and Loudon Hill: small in themselves, these victories kindled a ready movement in his support. And at this ripe moment word came from Cumberland that the fierce old Edward I, the 'Hammer of the Scots', was dead; in his place, Robert would have to contend with the languid and unwarlike son, King Edward II. While others hesitated, he launched expeditions to subdue Buchan at one end and Galloway at the other of what it was suddenly thinkable to call his kingdom.

In the half-dozen years that followed, Robert and his three like-minded generals – his brother Edward, Sir Thomas Randolph and James Douglas ('The Black') – perfected a native style of piecemeal guerrilla warfare that made a virtue of their lightness of armour. (An English chronicler's comment that after a skirmish of 1310 'Bruce fled in his usual manner' shows how systematically his strategy of raid and retreat had been applied.) Above all, partly from the experience of Wallace at Falkirk (1297), they had learned to avoid pitched battles, in which the English would generally enjoy the advantage in numbers (especially of cavalry) and equipment. If Bannockburn was Robert's greatest hour, it was also the exception to his chosen practice and principles.

The Scots had this battle thrust upon them by the impulsive nature of Edward Bruce. Besieging the English stronghold at Stirling, he made a deal with the governor to accept surrender in September 1314 if the town was not relieved by then. Edward II was thus honour-bound to raise an invading army, and Robert no less obliged to oppose him at Stirling. Edward made north with a force of at least 12,000 infantry and 2,000 cavalry; Robert had 5,000 foot-soldiers and no more than 500 light horse.

This gaping disparity in strength came home to the Scots as they watched the might of the English shimmering on the horizon: with its thousands of pennons waving and armour glittering in the June sunshine, it looked like an army descended from heaven. Yet, if it had to be a set-piece battle, the Scots had the advantage of choosing the ground to blunt the impact of English knights and archers. They could also look to their own innovations: the *schiltrom* – a hollow ring of men-at-arms, long spears bristling in all directions – had been designed as a defensive formation against cavalry attack, but under Wallace, and now Bruce, it had been redeveloped as a mobile unit which could mount potent attacks of its own. In addition, this was a battle whose preliminaries were to assume unusual significance.

Among the traditional exchanges on the day before the battle, which left the English smarting at unexpected losses, a vainglorious knight named Henry de Bohun happened to catch sight of the Bruce before his troops, lightly armed and mounted on a little grey pony, and charged at the opportunity. Robert, the Scots' champion as much as their king, recklessly faced the challenge, swerved suddenly to avoid de Bohun's lance, then – jumping up in his stirrups – struck with his battle-axe through the Englishman's basinet, splitting the head in two. The manoeuvre impressed all who saw it as an almost superhuman feat of arms. Robert had been unsure whether his army should stand and fight the next day, but his mind was made up by the damage dealt to English morale by that single blow.

Soon after dawn, the Scots advanced into prepared positions on a narrow front bordered by woods and marsh. The first wave of English cavalry, its horses plunging in concealed pits, failed to penetrate the hedge of Scottish spears, and the swirling chaos that ensued itself blocked further attacks. The vast numbers of the English infantry were unable to get at the enemy; and their redeployment was hampered by the course of several rivers. A crack force of Welsh archers, left with no protection against counterattack, was annihilated. The eruption of exultant Scottish camp followers from their cover on a nearby hill, waving banners made of branches and old clothes, looked to the dismayed invader like the arrival of a second Scottish army, and the tide of flight began. Many knights were captured for ransom; many more were slain with their soldiers on the banks or drowned in Bannock Burn; and Edward himself barely escaped, pursued through Lothian to Dunbar, where he scrambled aboard an open skiff and got off to Berwick.

This was the end, in practice, of English designs on the Scottish throne. As yet, while Edward declined to acknowledge Robert, Robert continued to lay waste his northern counties; and in the last decade of his life, Robert's tenacity began to yield constitutional fruit. In 1328 a third King Edward acknowledged him sovereign of an independent Scotland. Finally, on 13 June 1329, the Pope gave his blessing to the Scottish cause; though the Bruce himself, worn out by wars and disfigured by leprosy, had died, in his house by the Clyde, six days before the proclamation.

King Robert's body was buried in the abbey at Dunfermline; but not, by his own order, the heart, which was to be borne to the Holy Land in an act of pilgrimage he had been too embattled to achieve in his lifetime. The task was settled on his great comrade-in-arms James Douglas, who was seduced *en route* by an anti-Saracen action in southern Spain. Mortally wounded here, Douglas' dying act, we are told, was to fling his king's heart – itself belligerent beyond the last – into the teeth of the enemy. The heart was recovered and returned to Scotland, where it lies in the ruins of Melrose Abbey.

Rorke's Drift
Adrian Greaves

In 1879 Lord Chelmsford's disastrous invasion of Zululand and his unexpected defeat by the Zulu army at Isandlwana shook Victorian Britain. The nation desperately needed heroes, and the unprecedented award of 11 Victoria Crosses and five Distinguished Conduct Medals for the heroic defence of nearby Rorke's Drift ensured that an insignificant skirmish, bravely fought, transformed disaster into a great British victory. In 1964 the celebrated film *Zulu* immortalised the legend of tenacious Redcoats and dashing officers doggedly resisting overwhelming odds. The glory of the British Empire lived on.

On 11 January 1879 Lord Chelmsford led the British invasion force against Zululand, crossing the Buffalo River at the isolated Swedish mission station known as Rorke's Drift, temporarily co-opted as a military supply depot. This act of war against a friendly neighbour was unauthorised by the home government, but Chelmsford believed he could secure Zululand before news of his invasion reached England. Chelmsford's invasion force of 4,709 men advanced from Rorke's Drift, quietly nestling under the Oskarsberg Hill, and made camp ten miles inside Zululand at Isandlwana Hill prior to attacking the gathering Zulu army.

Rorke's Drift boasted two insignificant buildings – Surgeon Reynolds' temporary hospital with 30 patients and a storehouse containing the invading column's supplies – supported by Captain Stevenson with 300 black auxiliaries from Natal for labouring duties. On 22 January the detachment included Lieutenant Bromhead and 100 soldiers of 'B' Company 2/24th (Warwickshire) Regiment; his senior NCO was 24-year-old Colour Sergeant Bourne. An engineer officer, Lieutenant Chard, had arrived at Rorke's Drift the day before. All were under the command of Major Spalding.

After sunrise on 22 January Chard rode to nearby Isandlwana camp to ascertain his orders. Meanwhile, the Zulus had decoyed Chelmsford into believing the Zulu army was approaching Isandlwana and, overnight, Chelmsford marched half his force off to make battle. But the approaching Zulu army had slipped unobserved into a hidden valley three miles from the unprotected camp's flank. There were no orders for Chard, who observed massing Zulus advancing on the British position. He galloped back to Rorke's Drift, where he alerted Spalding; leaving Chard in command, Spalding set off to Helpmekaar for reinforcements declaring, 'nothing will happen, and I shall be back again this evening, early'. Reassured, Chard returned to his riverside tent for lunch without warning Bromhead, whose soldiers were avoiding the heat of the day by sleeping or haunting the cooking area.

Chelmsford's marching force was 12 miles from the unprepared British camp when the massed Zulu army attacked Isandlwana. Within two hours, the camp was destroyed and 1,400 troops lay massacred and disembowelled.

Led by Prince Dabulamanzi, the Zulu reserve of 4,500 Zulus then crossed into British Natal near Rorke's Drift and divided into raiding impis. One impi encountered Major

Spalding and forced his relief column back to Helpmekaar; another impi discovered the weakly defended mission station at Rorke's Drift. Alerted to the approaching Zulus, Bromhead urgently despatched a rider with a note to the garrison at Helpmekaar: 'Sir, Intelligence has just reached camp that the camp at Isandula Hill is taken by the enemy. Bromhead.' Bromhead organised a hastily erected defensive wall of mealie sacks and biscuit boxes, strengthened by two upturned wagons, between the storehouse and the hospital; the hospital was barricaded and loopholed for the anxiously awaiting soldiers to fire through. Colour Sergeant Bourne took a skirmishing party to delay the approaching Zulus. As the marauding Zulus approached Rorke's Drift, Captain Stevenson's terrified black auxiliaries deserted, hotly followed by Stevenson and his white NCOs. The men of 'B' Company fired a volley into the fleeing deserters and a Corporal Anderson fell dead. Bromhead hastily directed six soldiers to defend the hospital and sealed the doors and windows with sacks and boxes as the Zulus spread out into their classic attacking 'horns' formation, progressively forcing Bourne's skirmishers back to the post.

At 4.30 p.m. the Zulus charged the two buildings, only to be met by withering volley-fire from a hundred British rifles; many warriors fell during this concentrated charge. Those behind the Zulu casualties jumped over them, but their bravery was wasted as they were unable to climb the barricade, now awash with slippery blood. With no time to reload their rifles, the soldiers fought with their bayonets fixed and, although the Zulus relished close combat, forced their retreat. Such tactics were new to the soldiers, who were now fighting for their lives. Scores of dead and wounded Zulus soon lay several deep around the position.

Zulu marksmen commenced sniping into the backs of Bromhead's soldiers from the Oskarsberg, but they were poor shots and casualties were few. Close-range volleys blasted each Zulu attack, and those who survived could only run onto the waiting bloodied bayonets. Chard and Bromhead calmly controlled the outpost, and when a gap appeared one or the other would step forward to assist the fight, ensuring each wave of Zulus was forced to retreat. When Commissariat Officer Dalton was shot at close range, he handed his rifle to Chard before collapsing; Surgeon Reynolds dressed the wound and, within minutes, Dalton was back on his feet encouraging the defenders. Unable to reach the hospital, Reynolds bravely issued ammunition along the line.

Four of Chard's men were now seriously wounded, and one determined Zulu rush finally forced the soldiers to abandon the outer position and withdraw within the inner wall of boxes next to the storehouse. Chard could no longer communicate with those trapped in the hospital, 40 yards away and surrounded by Zulus.

A soldier shouted that he saw marching Redcoats approaching from Helpmekaar. Some of the men cheered, which confused the Zulus. They momentarily withdrew but, when no relieving troops came, regrouped for the next assault. Chard wrote of this incident: 'It is very strange that this report should have arisen amongst us, for the two companies [sic]

Overleaf: *Heroism against the odds: Rorke's Drift produced 11 Victoria Crosses and 5 Distinguished Conduct Medals*

24th Regiment from Helpmekaar did come down to the foot of the hill, but not, I believe, in sight of us. They marched back to Helpmekaar on the report of Rorke's Drift having fallen.' With darkness falling, the Zulus attacked the hospital's barricaded doors and windows, grabbing at the soldiers' rifles as they fired through the loopholes. Then the hospital caught fire: Private Hook wrote, 'We were like rats in a trap'. The Zulus began clawing at the barricaded doors, forcing the defenders through to the far room, its high window overlooking Chard's position. In the glare of the hospital flames Chard saw the defenders lowering the patients to the ground. The Zulus were only yards away when Chard ordered covering fire and called for volunteers to bring the patients to safety. Although wounded, Private Hitch and Corporal Allen immediately volunteered; the two raced to and from the hospital, each time carrying a patient. The hospital was quickly vacated; the terrifying battle in the darkness, thick smoke and deafening noise had lasted over two hours.

The final desperate fight for survival now began. Drawn by the flames and sounds of constant firing, Zulu reinforcements arrived. Facing imminent death, and with hand-to-hand fighting around them, a dozen weary soldiers constructed a final redoubt of mealie sacks. The wounded were placed inside the 'last post' position and Chard detailed marksmen to occupy the upper rampart. Eventually, the Zulus' enthusiasm for close combat waned, and after midnight their attacks reduced to half-hearted probes. Prince Dabulamanzi's men had suffered enormous casualties with nothing to show for their undisputed bravery. At dawn the exhausted Zulus collected themselves together and, leaving over 300 of their warriors dead, retreated towards Zululand.

The soldiers were all suffering from bruising and burns caused by constantly firing their Martini-Henry rifles. Pools of congealed blood bore witness to the death-throes of both sides, and the whole area was littered with bodies, spears, empty ammunition boxes and clusters of spent ammunition cases. The soldiers contemplated the Zulu dead, sometimes five deep; dying and wounded warriors were given the *coup de grâce* by bayonet; there was no malice – neither side took prisoners.

At 9.00 a.m. Chelmsford and his survivors reached Rorke's Drift, where 'the occupants received the General with three cheers'. Chelmsford and his staff were shocked by the carnage that greeted them. Hundreds of bodies lay around the mission station and within the burnt-out hospital building. Chelmsford thanked the survivors for their endeavours before departing to report the defeat of his force and the annihilation of a famous British regiment.

After the tragedy of Isandlwana, Chelmsford described the survival of Rorke's Drift as a 'gleam of sunshine'. But if, encouraged by the popular press, Chelmsford and the politicians successfully used victory at Rorke's Drift to neutralise defeat at Isandlwana, the Army viewed it as only a minor skirmish. News of awards provoked annoyance through the ranks and contempt from General Wolseley, Chelmsford's successor, from which many survivors would later suffer. Both Chard and Bromhead were promoted, but their careers subsequently floundered. But it is they and their heroic co-defenders who won the battle for posterity. Today, Rorke's Drift ranks as one of the most popular British battlefields in the world.

The Royal Marines
Julian Thompson

The Royal Marines are one of the most famous military forces in the world. Their achievements, toughness, professionalism and enterprise put them in the same league as other élites such as the SAS, the Paras, the US Marines and the French Foreign Legion. Like the Foreign Legion, they gained their reputation after years of gruelling service in far corners of the world, often unseen and unheard, and too frequently unappreciated.

The Royal Marines trace their descent from a regiment specially raised and trained for service with the Navy by Charles II in 1664. The regiment was named the Duke of York's Maritime Regiment of Foot after their first colonel, the Lord High Admiral, Charles' brother James Duke of York. Defined as 'land souldjers', their arrival was welcomed by James, because it would bring personal loyalty and discipline to the fleet. At that time, and for years afterwards, ships' crews were 'paid off' in peacetime, and impressed or recruited from volunteers from the seafaring population in war. Only the Marines were in regular service.

In action, the Marines provided trained and disciplined troops stationed on the quarterdeck and poop of their own ship and in the fighting tops, able to bring down fire on an enemy ship's upper decks. Marines also led boarding parties and repelled enemy boarders. Although seamen played their part in this fighting, in battle they were usually employed manning the 'great guns' or working the ship and had to be taken from these tasks to join boarding parties or assist in repelling boarders, whereas the Marines were a force under the captain's hand, immediately ready for any eventuality. Marines also took part in landing operations and capturing enemy ships, usually under cover of darkness when their quarry was in port or at anchor, known at the time as 'cutting out'. Sometimes when needed the Marines would land in battalion or greater strength for protracted fighting ashore.

The Marines took part in all the great naval battles of the age of sail right up to the end of the Napoleonic Wars, and in many ashore. The exploits of Edward 'Fighting' Nicholls illustrate the variety of life of a Marine officer of the early 19th century. In 1803 Nicholls volunteered to lead a cutting-out expedition, and with only 13 men took the French cutter *Albion*, his second such foray that year. In 1804 he led a landing party in the Dardanelles, burning a Turkish frigate, storming a redoubt and spiking the guns. His actions allowed the British fleet to pass through the Dardanelles, a feat that eluded their successors in World War I. In 1809 he led the force that captured the Danish island of Anholt, and during the war of 1812 against the Americans Nicholls, with 70 Marines, formed a force of Creek and Choctaw Indians in eastern Louisiana to draw off troops defending New Orleans. He was in action 107 times, wounded six times and court-martialled twice, but survived to be knighted and promoted full general.

After the Napoleonic Wars, the Royal (since 1802) Marines were given the badge they wear today, the globe surrounded by the laurel wreath. The globe was chosen by King

JOIN THE ROYAL MARINES

Help to man the guns of the Fleet

W. H. SMITH & SON, PRINTERS, 55 FETTER LANE, LONDON, E.C.

George IV in 1827 to represent the 109 battle honours already earned by the Royal Marines – more than could fit on their colours. The Marines served in numerous campaigns throughout Queen Victoria's reign, but by the end of the 19th century the Navy had changed beyond recognition. Steam-driven warships, long-range gunnery and changes in tactics meant that 'cutting-out' and boarding parties were no longer needed.

In World War I the Royal Marines gave sterling service in the major warships – at Jutland, for example, some 6,000 served in the Grand Fleet. Major Harvey saved Admiral Beatty's flagship, the *Lion*, from certain destruction when, although dying with both legs blown off, he ordered the flooding of his turret's magazine. He was posthumously awarded the Victoria Cross. Royal Marine battalions saw their hardest fighting with the Royal Naval Division at Gallipoli and in France and Flanders. At Gallipoli they fought alongside the Australians, and after one battle the Australian VC Captain Quinn said to one of the officers of the Royal Marine Brigade, 'the bravest thing I've seen so far was the charge of your two battalions up that hill on Bloody Sunday'. One of the most highly decorated Marines in France was F. W. Lumsden. Starting as a major, he rose to brigadier general and, in addition to three DSOs, was awarded the VC. He was killed while leading his brigade.

A Royal Marine battalion also played the leading role ashore in the great raid on Zeebrugge in April 1918. There were so many acts of gallantry that night that all ranks were balloted in order to decide to whom the VC should be awarded.

In World War II the Royal Marines took on the tasks familiar to us today: the commandos, the landing craft and the small raiding forces that eventually after the war became the Special Boat Service (SBS). Throughout the war the Royal Marines saw much action in their traditional role at sea, but also served in a division that saw no fighting. Lord Mountbatten, then Chief of Combined Operations, recognised that this was a waste of great talent and the division was disbanded to form commandos and landing craft crews in time for the great amphibious operations of 1942 and later. The Royal Marines raised nine commandos, manned large numbers of landing craft, and fought in the forefront of battles in Sicily, Italy, the Adriatic, France, Holland, Germany and Burma.

Some 17,500 Marines took part in the Normandy landings, and by the end more than 25,000 were involved in the liberation of north-west Europe. In the landing on Walcheren Island in the Scheldt estuary, Marines manning support landing craft closed and engaged the German defences to cover their Marine commando comrades approaching the beach. Of the 25 support craft only four remained fit for action. Their self-sacrifice in drawing the fire of the batteries was not in vain. Casualties among the landing craft and commandos during the run-in of the first two waves were light.

The feats of the Royal Marine commandos in World War II ensured the survival of the Marines in the face of severe cuts following the end of the fighting. For them, like the rest of the British armed services, the end of the war marked the start of a period of almost continuous action covering the 60 years to the present day. It has not ended yet. The Royal

'The greatest corps in the world': a World War I recruitment poster for the Royal Marines

Marines served in the counter-insurgency operations in Palestine; in the jungles of Malaya; and in Korea with the 1st United States Marine Division in the great battle of the Chosin Reservoir, subsequently raiding the enemy lines of communication. They served in the Canal Zone in Egypt and in Cyprus against General Grivas, and spearheaded the amphibious landings at Suez. They fought in the mountainous jungles of Borneo and on the rugged mountain frontier of Aden, and served many tours of duty in Northern Ireland. Marines played their part in the First Gulf War, northern Iraq, Sierra Leone and Bosnia. But for the amphibious expertise of the Royal Marines, any landings on the Falkland Islands in 1982 would have been impossible. Their contribution to the subsequent fighting was absolutely crucial: without them the Falkland Islands would still be under Argentine rule. In Afghanistan in 2001 the Royal Marine commandos provided the only troops with the skills needed to take on the Taliban in their formidable mountains; after the first encounter, the Taliban decided not to tangle with them and fled to Pakistan. The Special Boat Service was largely responsible for the capture of Masir-e-Sharif. Royal Marines also supported other Special Forces operations in Afghanistan. They spearheaded the British operation in Iraq, and fought a brilliant campaign to open the way for the capture of Basra. Royal Marines also supported Special Forces in western Iraq.

The unofficial motto of the French Foreign Legion, loosely translated as 'get yourself out of trouble because no one else is going to', could equally have applied to the Royal Marines in the 340 years of what Winston Churchill called their 'long, rough, glorious history': on the bullet-swept decks of ships under sail, in the turrets of warships in both world wars, closing the enemy-held coastline in landing craft, wading ashore with the cold sea behind and potential disaster staring them in the face, in helicopters, landing craft and amphibians of many kinds, and in the end so often in what someone called 'leather personnel carriers' – boots – 'yomping' under a heavy load to close with and engage the enemy. Not for nothing did Churchill call them 'the greatest corps in the world'.

The war reporting of William Howard Russell
Phillip Knightley

William Howard Russell pioneered the craft of modern war reporting, an immense leap in the history of journalism. 'I am the miserable parent of a luckless tribe,' was his own description of this achievement.

Before Russell, an Irish reporter on *The Times*, arrived on the scene in 1854, British newspapers either copied war reports from foreign newspapers or employed junior army officers to send reports from the front. Neither system worked well. Reports in foreign newspapers were unreliable, biased and late. British officers understandably put their military duties ahead of their reporting duties, had little idea of what constituted news and had no sense of urgency. So when war broke out between Britain and Russia in 1854 over Russia's desire to expand her empire, *The Times* decided it would have to find a new way of satisfying the desire of an increasingly literate public for news. The war was immensely popular and *The Times*' manager noted, 'The public expects that we shall have our own agents'. The newspaper therefore decided to send Russell, an enterprising general journalist, to accompany the British troops, first to Malta and, when this worked well, to the front.

Russell was well equipped for the assignment. He had been attracted to military life as a boy and used to get up early to watch soldiers drilling at his local barracks. He had tried several times to enlist, but his grandfather stopped him. He had considered becoming a doctor, but when his cousin was sent by *The Times* to cover the Irish elections he hired Russell to help him and in no time Russell was hooked – he realised that journalism was his métier. His cunning, persistence, initiative and solid reporting caught the attention of *The Times*' editor, John Delane, who hired him. So in April 1854 Russell found himself a war correspondent – that is, an independent civilian reporter sent to the front to tell the public back home how the war was going.

He quickly realised that the answer was: not well. The British Army had not fought a war since Wellington had beaten Napoleon at Waterloo some 40 years earlier. There was no single War Office, and the command was dominated by noble blood. The expedition leader, Lord Raglan, was 65 and, although he had had a distinguished military career, had never commanded so much as a battalion in the field. The low-ranking officers seemed to regard the war as a picnic – they brought a French chef, native servants, their favourite horses and wine, their shotguns, dogs and wives. Russell could not believe that the British were serious, and in one of his early despatches he said so:

> The management is infamous and the contrast offered by our proceedings to the conduct of the French [Britain's ally] most painful. Could you believe it – the sick have not a bed to lie upon. They are landed and thrown into a rickety house without

a chair or a table in it. The French with their ambulances, excellent commissariat staff and boulangerie etc, in every respect are immeasurably our superiors.

Russell then set out the dilemma that sooner or later confronts most war correspondents: whose side was he on? He was a British correspondent accompanying a British Army fighting what he believed was a justified war. He wanted Britain to win. But the big story was undoubtedly the Army's incompetence, and if he wrote it would he not, in effect, be helping the Russians, the enemy? He passed the problem to his editor, Delane: 'Am I to tell these things, or hold my tongue?' Delane replied: 'Continue to tell the truth, as much of it as you can, and leave such comment as may be dangerous to us.' And then, as is an editor's privilege, Delane took it upon himself to decide which of Russell's despatches he would use in *The Times*. Those he considered too provocative he nevertheless circulated privately to Cabinet ministers, beginning a process that was eventually to topple the government.

Russell's reporting technique – since he realised he could not be everywhere at once – was to go around the front interviewing anyone who would talk to him and asking for impressions. Sometimes he was lucky enough to be at the right spot at a crucial moment. So from a hill overlooking Balaclava he watched the disastrous Charge of the Light Brigade – of the 673 men who rode at the Russian guns fewer than 200 returned. Appalled, Russell wrote in his diary: 'I looked at the group of officers representing the military mind of England close at hand in this crisis and I was not much impressed with confidence by what I saw.' But, anxious not to appear defeatist, his report for *The Times* concentrated on the bravery and glory of such a suicidal charge. Russell could not keep it up. He wrote to Delane on 17 January 1855: 'Let no one at home attempt to throw dirt in your eyes. This army is to all intents and purposes … used up, destroyed and ruined … My occupation is gone; there is nothing to record more of the British expedition except its weakness and its misery.'

Raglan could ignore Russell no longer. He got the Deputy Judge-Advocate to claim that Russell's despatches had involved serious breaches of security and had afforded assistance to the enemy. This was probably true. In one article alone, published in *The Times* on 23 October 1854, Russell revealed how many artillery pieces had been moved to the front, the position and amount of gunpowder needed to supply them, the exact position of two regiments and the fact that there was a dearth of roundshot (though after the war the Russian commander said he never learnt anything from *The Times* that he had not already been told by his spies). But it was too late for Raglan. Public opinion was against him, and when *The Times* used Russell's reports to demand Raglan's recall the government succumbed, railing to the last against Russell and his reporting. When the Duke of Newcastle, the new Secretary for War, came to the Crimea in the spring of 1855 he told Russell: 'It was you who turned out the Government.'

Russell returned to London and fame. *The Times* put him on its list of foreign correspondents at £600 a year, a huge salary in those days. He had breakfast with the Prime

W. H. Russell, father of modern war reporting, by Roger Fenton, father of war photography

Minister, Lord Palmerston, who, mistakenly believing that Russell's criticisms of the conduct of the war must have been inspired by his having constructive alternatives, disconcerted Russell by asking him what he would do if he were commander-in-chief of the Army. His despatches were published in book form, and while awaiting new wars he went on a lecture tour. Then in 1857 he went off to India to cover the Indian Mutiny. There his war reporting showed a much sharper and more liberal perception of the issues than either his colleagues or his newspaper. While *The Times* was advocating bloody revenge against the Sepoys and their leaders, Russell saw that Britain's days in India were numbered: 'The Anglo-Saxons must either abate their strong natural feeling against the coloured race … or look forward to the day … when the indulgence of their passions will render the government of India too costly a luxury for the English people.'

From India he went to America, where he dined with Lincoln, who put the Union case to him. He then went off on a tour of the South, where a first-hand study of the slave market disgusted him. The outbreak of the Civil War thus found him deeply attached to the Union cause and with a high opinion of Lincoln's motives – a stance not in keeping with the pro-Southern editorial line of *The Times*. Unhappy, Russell went to Canada for a few weeks' break. *The Times* was furious. 'You must either go to the front or come home,' the foreign manager telegraphed to him. 'Up to the beginning of this year you did well, but since then you seem to have lost heart and to have thrown us overboard.' Russell packed up and returned to Britain, where *The Times* retired him with a modest pension. Russell explained: 'As I from the first maintained that the North must win, I was tabooed from dealing with American questions in The Times even after my return to England but en revanche, I have had my say in the Army and Navy Gazette, which I have bought.'

The best of Russell's career was behind him. He reappeared briefly for *The Times* in the Franco-Prussian war, but could not adapt his despatches to the demand for crisp, concise, factual reports prompted by the increasing use of the telegraph. He was persuaded to accompany a British expedition to South Africa in 1879, but an accident with his horse left him lame and he never covered another war. He died in 1907, convinced that the war correspondent's best days were over and that increasing military censorship had killed the craft he himself had virtually invented. It was a rival correspondent, Edwin Godkin of the *Daily News*, who best summed up his importance. Russell had, he said, brought home to governments the fact that the people had something to say about wars and that 'they should not be the concern exclusively of sovereigns and statesmen'.

Flora Sandes
Kate Adie

She cut an unlikely military figure. A 38-year-old spinster setting out for Serbia, pride of place in her luggage given to two hot water bottles, insect powder and a violin.

Flora Sandes, a rector's daughter from Suffolk, had responded immediately to the call for medical volunteers in the first week of World War I, but she was less than confident about what she could contribute, possessing only a clutch of St John Ambulance certificates and a boundless sense of optimism. She was not in the tradition of those women who disguised themselves in order to join the military; indeed, she hadn't a thought in her head about becoming a soldier. However, there was an adventurous streak in her nature – she'd crossed to America after a marriage proposal from a naval officer, only to dump him when confronted with small-town society, then bicycled through Central America to visit one of her brothers working on the Panama Canal. Her attitude to an Edwardian woman's place was: 'if you have the misfortune to be born a woman it is better to make the best of a bad job, and not try to be a bad imitation of a man'.

The flurry of patriotism, anxiety and excitement which produced thousands of volunteers immediately after the declaration of war in 1914 included a huge number of women – who found that the authorities were not particularly interested in them. Undeterred, possessing years of experience in charitable and voluntary bodies – and with a backbone of suffrage campaigning – women like Flora organised themselves for 'war work'.

They had no idea what lay ahead of them. First Aid training didn't prepare them for the hundreds of thousands of mutilated victims of the Great War. Flora set off with six other nursing volunteers supervised by a 26-year-old American, Madame Grouitch, who was married to a Serbian politician. The first four months were spent just behind the lines in a grim military hospital in Kragujevac, so filthy and ill-equipped that Flora sailed back to London and raised an immense sum for necessary supplies. On her return, a typhus epidemic was killing Serbian soldiers, Austrian prisoners of war and the medical staff. The First Aider found herself wielding a knife and performing amputations. Her skill with the bone-saw managed to overcome military prejudice, for it was highly unusual for women, even in Britain, to be allowed to practice surgery. Elsewhere in Serbia, especially in the impressively run Scottish Women's Hospitals, several doctors who'd been refused posts in the Army Medical Service or barred from surgical training found themselves faced with boundless, if appalling, opportunities to fulfil their ambitions.

In autumn 1915 the Serb army was torn into by the combined forces of Austria, Germany and Bulgaria, and began a long and horrific retreat over the mountains to Montenegro and Albania. Flora was with an ambulance unit – but not for long: 'When the

Overleaf: *The only British woman to fight in World War I: Flora Sandes in Salonica, 1916*

Brigade holding Baboona Pass began slowly to retreat towards Albania, where there were no roads, and we could take no ambulances to carry the sick, I took the red cross off my arm and said, very well, I would join the 2nd Infantry as a private.'

Her acceptance into the ranks was partly based on her nationality: the Serb officers were highly receptive to the notion of a representative of one of their allies offering to fight alongside them. Flora might have been a woman and have something of her father's Irish accent, but the symbolism of a gesture from the British was powerful as the Serbs faced annihilation. She could also ride and shoot, speak French, German and passable Serbo-Croat, and lived without complaint in the worst operational conditions.

The epic mountain journey left corpses littering the snow: hundreds of thousands – soldiers, prisoners, conscripted boys, women and children – perished. There were skirmishes too, and Private Sandes showed that she'd no problems levelling a rifle at the enemy. She'd found her true vocation. Not an aggressive woman, she nevertheless believed passionately in the cause she was serving, and she loved her comrades. She was intelligent and sophisticated enough to deal with the anomalies of her position: there were a number of peasant girls in the Serbian army, but her presence as 'an English lady' was clearly conspicuous. Good-looking, her hair whitened by typhus, with well-tailored jacket and breeches and an exuberant personality, she slept alongside her unit and employed commonsense and good humour to deal with sexual approaches. She intended to be worthy of respect and trusted as a soldier, reacting sharply to the suggestion that she should revert to being a nurse: as a soldier, she pointed out, she behaved as a soldier, caring for the wounded only 'between shots'.

For the rest of the war she shared the privations and dangers of her unit, earning promotion to corporal, then to sergeant. She was given a batman and a horse, but was grateful for, rather than embarrassed by, these unusual privileges. The rigours of warfare were treated in a matter-of-fact manner in her letters and diaries:

> We all wear those iron helmets; I hate mine when it is very hot, but love it when we get shelled, which happens pretty often, with very slight cover, and stones and shrapnel come pattering down on it; I only wish on those occasions it was big enough to crawl right under like a snail's shell.

She took part in close-quarter combat, and came to know the Serbo-Croat for 'fix bayonets'. Though she never denied her fear, her colleagues thought her courageous. Describing her injuries sustained in the attack on Monastir in 1916, she remarks conversationally:

> I daresay you've heard that I got knocked out by a Bulgar hand-bomb, so I never got into Monastir after all; but I've had a very good run for my money all the same, as I had three months' incessant fighting without a scratch … The Serbs are fine comrades. We thought once we should all get taken, but they wouldn't leave me! I've had ever so

many cards from them asking when I'm coming back, but as I have twenty-four
wounds and a broken arm the doctors seem to think I'll have to wait a bit.'

Fortunately, she'd been hauled off the battlefield by two comrades: when they returned to
the spot where she'd been wounded, they found 12 of her unit with their throats cuts, laid
out neatly in a row.

The country's highest military award, the Karageorge Star, was awarded to her while
she was in her hospital bed; however, she returned to active service with 'half a blacksmith's
shop' still inside her, and spent months engaged in trench warfare and raiding.

When the war ended, Flora stayed in the army for a further three years and –
confounding any gossip about her sexuality – fell in love with a fellow officer, Yuri
Yudenitch. They married and travelled extensively, settling for a time in Paris, where
Flora employed her military discipline as chaperone and wardrobe mistress at the Folies
Bergères, before returning to Belgrade.

World War II saw her called up as a reservist, so off she went at the age of 64, into
uniform again, only to be taken prisoner by the Nazis and held in a military hospital. Flora
merely waited for the visit of a friend, who brought a bundle of women's clothes. She
changed and then walked out – no one, of course, noticing a mere woman. She was
rearrested briefly, but treated with respect for the rest of the war, for her reputation in Serbia
was considerable, even among the Germans. In 1945, by now a widow, the RAF flew her
home to England, and she spent her last years in Suffolk, proud of her revolver, her sword
and her medals.

As a voice for Serbia during World War I, Flora Sandes was unrivalled: her frequent
fundraising tours drew huge audiences, and she spoke with first-hand frontline experience.
Headlines described her as 'The Serbian Joan of Arc' and she aroused admiration and not a
little amazement. Touring Australia in 1920, she epitomised the newly liberated woman:
cropped hair, army uniform, smoking in public.

She was the only British woman to have fought officially in World War I, but she never
thought of herself as a 'heroic oddity'. Her military service had been logical and satisfying,
and, bolstered by a sincere passion for the Serbs' cause, she had loved the companionship,
the variety, the intensity of being part of the military world. She did not find it dramatic to
turn from nurse to soldier; rather the reverse, as she recalled when back in Suffolk: 'I cannot
attempt to describe what it now felt like, trying to get accustomed to a woman's life and a
woman's clothes again; and also to ordinary society after having lived entirely with men for
so many years. Turning from a woman to a private soldier was nothing compared with
turning back from soldier to ordinary woman.'

The SAS
William Fowler

At 7.23 p.m. the frame charge exploded, blasting in the first-floor front window of the Iranian Embassy at 16 Prince's Gate, Kensington, London. It was Monday 5 May 1980, and the Blue and Red Teams from the 22 Special Air Service (SAS) Regiment's specialist anti-terrorist 'Pagoda' Troop were storming the building where for six days six Iraqi-backed Arab terrorists had held 26 hostages and killed one.

In 17 minutes the SAS team rescued all the hostages. Part of the operation was caught live on national and international television, since TV cameras had been in position in Kensington Gardens to cover the developing hostage drama. Until that evening the SAS' reputation for very high selection standards and military professionalism in the field had largely been limited to within the British Army, where they were known to many simply as 'The Super Soldiers'. The operation, codenamed 'Nimrod', would put the SAS in the public eye, and subsequent actions around the world ensure that this formerly secretive force would always be front-page news.

The SAS was founded during World War II, in Egypt in 1941. It was the brainchild of two young officers, Lieutenants David Stirling and Jock Lewes, who put together a small unit with 66 volunteers to conduct raids against the enemy forces facing the British Army in the Western Desert. In its first two years alone the growing force destroyed 400 German aircraft, largely the Ju 52 transport planes that were critical to the supply and reinforcement of Axis forces in North Africa.

An officer who had been tasked with strategic deception by the HQ in Cairo had selected the name. The idea for the airborne unit had been developed following the battle of Sidi Barrani in December 1940, when the captured diary of an Italian officer had revealed fears that the British paratroops might land behind Axis lines. The distinctive cap badge and parachute wings that the group devised helped foster the illusion that a large airborne force had been deployed to North Africa. From 1943 the SAS operated behind German lines in Italy and France, and became a very effective reconnaissance screen for the advancing Allied forces in Belgium, Holland and Germany in 1945.

Like the Army Commandos, the SAS was disbanded at the close of the war. After campaigning by wartime veterans it was retained as a reserve formation within the Territorial Army, with the title 21 SAS – which brought together the titles of the wartime regiments of 1 and 2 SAS. However, the need for Special Forces to conduct long-range patrols deep in the jungle of Malaya against Communist guerrillas led to the reestablishment of a regular SAS regiment, which became 22 SAS. In Malaya, where operations lasted from 1948 to 1960, the SAS were inserted deep into the jungle by

'The Super Soldiers': SAS men storm the Iranian Embassy in London, May 1980

parachute and patrolled for weeks. It was during this period that the C Squadron was formed, made up of soldiers from the colonies of North and South Rhodesia. Following Rhodesia's unilateral declaration of independence (UDI) in 1965, C Squadron played a key role in operations against insurgents. It was disbanded in 1980 following independence and majority rule.

In 1956 the SAS were sent to Aden to help counter local armed opposition to British rule in Yemen, where they fought in the tough mountainous terrain in the north of the colony; and between 1962 and 1966 cross-border attacks by Indonesia against the states of Sarawak and Sabah, part of the newly formed Malaysian Federation, led to the deployment of SAS squadrons in cross-border operations against the bases from which the Indonesians were, in their own words, 'confronting' the Federation. The SAS built up an excellent relationship with the jungle tribes in a 'hearts and minds' operation that yielded valuable intelligence about Indonesian operations. It was during the Confrontation that New Zealand and Australian SAS troops – formed in 1954 and 1957 respectively – saw action for the first time. They would subsequently fight in Vietnam, mounting patrols and ambushes deep inside Viet Cong-controlled territory.

The climax of 22 SAS operations in the war that lasted from 1970 to 1976 in Oman, where Marxist-inspired insurgents were seeking to topple the British-backed Sultanate, was at the coastal town of Mirbat in 1972. Here, on 19 July, a band of nine SAS men in a small fort held off attacks by around 400 well-armed insurgents.

In 1982 the Argentine military junta launched an attack that captured the British colony of the Falkland Islands. In the brief war that followed, SAS successes included the seizure of Mount Kent, an area of strategically important terrain covering approaches to the capital Stanley. Earlier D Squadron 22 SAS had made their way to an Argentine-controlled landing strip at Pebble Island on West Falkland, where they proceeded to destroy 11 enemy aircraft with demolition charges.

In the First Gulf War of 1991, following the Iraqi invasion of Kuwait, the SAS had several missions, one of which was to gather intelligence on the movement of Iraqi troop and weapons convoys. To do this they set up roadwatch patrols on three points on the three east-west axes. The teams drawn from B Squadron were inserted by helicopter about 225 to 290 km inside Iraq. There were also four vehicle-mounted fighting columns of up to a dozen Land Rovers, each column with a German-built Unimog truck loaned from the Saudis as a support vehicle. Two columns came from A Squadron and two from D. One of their missions was to locate the Iraqi Scud surface-to-surface missiles that were being launched against neighbouring states like Saudi Arabia and the neutral Israel.

In 1994 the SAS mounted a rescue operation to locate a group of British soldiers who had been lost for a month in the mountain jungles of Borneo. The same year, an SAS man was reported to have been killed in Gorazde, revealing the force's involvement in the Bosnian conflict in former Yugoslavia. Again, D Squadron 22 SAS were employed in a heliborne rescue operation in September 2000 in the West African state of Sierra Leone, where a group of British soldiers had been held hostage by a heavily armed local gang.

In 2001 the SAS deployed to Afghanistan, gathering intelligence about the possible hiding place of Osama bin Laden, the Saudi-born leader of al-Qaeda. Working with men of the Australian SAS and US Special Forces, they attacked locations where Taliban or al-Qaeda forces had established bases and depots. In the Second Gulf War in 2003 SAS patrols working ahead of the US-led coalition forces collaborated with the Australian SAS and US Special Forces to seize key points inside Iraq to assist the advance of the major land forces.

All soldiers in the SAS are volunteers who have had previous service with a corps or regiment within the British, Australian or New Zealand armies and so are men in their mid-twenties to early thirties. Volunteers go through Selection Training, a one-month course developed in 1953 following experience in Malaya. It is designed to weed out unsuitable soldiers by testing stamina, endurance and mental strength. It is run twice a year and in the UK takes place over the Brecon Beacons in Wales. The culmination is the 'Long Drag' where, working individually, volunteers carrying 25 kg rucksacks navigate round a 60 km course in 20 hours.

After he has passed Selection the volunteer has 14 weeks of Continuation Training in which he learns the skills that will make him an effective member of the four-man patrol – the basic unit of the SAS. The next phase is four to six weeks of Jungle Training in Brunei, where four-man patrols undertake test missions. If volunteers fail Jungle Training they are Returned to Unit (RTU'd). Finally, volunteers attend the four-week Static-Line Parachute Course, unless they are soldiers in the Parachute Regiment. At the end of the course the volunteers are awarded their distinctive 'sabre' wings and return to the SAS depot where they are 'badged', receiving the distinctive sand-coloured beret with its winged sword cap badge.

Not surprisingly, before this expense of time and effort by the SAS Training Wing the Army requires a commitment that the volunteer will serve a minimum of three years and three months. Soldiers remain with 22 SAS and progress through the rank structure, but after serving for some years officers will return to their parent regiment, taking their experience and energy back into the mainstream of the Army.

Since their beginnings in North Africa the SAS have become the yardstick by which the Special Forces of the world are judged. In 1941 Stirling and Lewes had set their standards:

Engage in the never-ending pursuit of excellence.
Maintain the highest standards of self-discipline in all aspects of daily life.
Tolerate no sense of class, all ranks in the SAS belong to one company.
All ranks to possess humility and humour.

For all the media attention and myths that the SAS has attracted since that evening at the Iranian Embassy in May 1980, serving and former soldiers are by and large modest men who out of uniform have been mistaken for farmers, sports coaches, even university academics – Super Soldiers on duty only.

Viscount Slim
Julian Thompson

Mid-March 1942: the British are retreating from the invading Japanese in Burma. The seaport of Rangoon has fallen. The British troops are cut off from the sea. There is nowhere to go but back to India 900 miles away. Into this slough of despond steps a new commander, Lieutenant-General William Slim, to take over what was known as The Burma Corps, or Burcorps.

The Japanese had air superiority. Their soldiers were better trained, and by moving across country had the apparently uncanny knack of being able to cut in behind the road-bound British troops with their masses of wheeled transport. Although the British and Indian soldiers of Burcorps made many a gallant stand, they were inexorably forced back. Yet Slim never lost heart. All who saw him spoke of his calm and good humour, his fortitude in the face of desperate danger. His robber-baron face, hard mouth, bulldog chin and force of personality inspired confidence. A soldier's soldier, he talked cheerfully to his troops in English, Gurkhali and Urdu, inspiring them by his presence. As an officer of the Indian Army, he was fluent in all three languages.

From a middle-class background in Birmingham, Slim was commissioned into the Warwickshire Regiment at the start of World War I. He was wounded at Gallipoli and in Mesopotamia (present-day Iraq), where he was awarded the Military Cross. After the war he transferred to the 6th Gurkha Rifles in the Indian Army. He passed out top from the Staff College at Quetta, and was subsequently selected to fill the only Indian Army vacancy on the staff of the British Army Staff College at Camberley. He commanded a brigade in the conquest of Abyssinia, where he was wounded again, and the 10th Indian Division in the campaign against the Vichy French in Syria and later in Iraq. It was from here that he was plucked out to command Burcorps.

Now, at the end of the longest retreat in the history of the British Army, Slim stood watching the emaciated, malaria-ridden rearguard of his corps march into India. The monsoon had burst upon them a few days before. The tracks were inches deep in slippery mud. The nights were bitterly cold, and few had blankets to cover them as they lay under the dripping trees. The monsoon brought one blessing: it stopped the Japanese following up and grounded their air force. In no small measure, though, the British owed their survival to Slim, who wrote later: 'as they trudged in behind the surviving officers in groups pitifully small they still carried their arms and kept their ranks, they were still recognizable as fighting units. They might look like scarecrows but they looked like soldiers too.'

Burcorps was broken up, and Slim took over 15th Corps, expecting to take command of the campaign in the Arakan. But General Irwin, the Army Commander, decided to control

Field Marshal Sir William Slim outside Fourteenth Army HQ in Burma, March 1945

it himself. He did not do well, and the offensive on which Churchill had pinned much hope ground to a halt within sight of the objective, and ended back where it had started. Slim's advice was sought by Irwin, and ignored. Eventually Slim was sent to the Arakan to sort out the mess. Here he implemented the only practicable solution: to pull even further back and fight on ground of his choosing. Irwin was furious and recommended that Slim be sacked. But major changes were afoot, and Irwin was relieved instead. He sent a signal to Slim saying, 'You're not sacked, I am'.

Slim was given command of the newly formed Fourteenth Army and set about preparing for the next offensive. His plan was to advance with the 15th Corps in the Arakan, and subsequently further north with the 4th and 3rd Corps from Assam, across the Chindwin. Needless to say, the Japanese were planning too. They decided to attack in the Arakan to draw off reserves from Assam, where they planned their main offensive. As the 15th Corps offensive gathered momentum in the Arakan, the Japanese struck, cutting off a large part of the 7th Indian Division. The Japanese propaganda radio announcer Tokyo Rose exulted: 'Why not go home? It's all over in Burma.' 'Actually,' wrote Slim, 'it was just beginning.' Instead of retreating, as they would have done in the past, the British and Indian soldiers held firm and were supplied by air as Slim had promised. Eventually the Japanese reeled back, having failed to capture the supplies on which they were relying for success.

In Assam the Japanese attacked earlier than Slim expected, but in a classic fighting withdrawal the 17th Indian Division pulled back to the key supply base at Imphal, avoiding being cut off while inflicting a bloody nose on the Japanese. Further north, the Japanese nearly succeeded in capturing Kohima, a vital intermediate base on the lines of communication through Assam and on to India. Again the Japanese gambled on capturing supplies to sustain their offensive. But they had played into Slim's hands. He was fighting them on the ground he had chosen, where he could supply and support his two corps and use his air power to the maximum effect.

The fighting round Imphal and Kohima was bitter and lasted for five months. Although under pressure from the Supreme Commander South East Asia, Lord Mountbatten, Slim was unflustered and refused to take operational shortcuts to attempt to push the Japanese back earlier than he deemed practical. He respected the fighting quality of the Japanese far too highly to take such liberties. By the end of 1944, after a bitterly contested advance, the Fourteenth Army was back on the Chindwin from where they had withdrawn earlier in the year. The Japanese paid dearly: of some 85,000 who marched on Assam, half died in battle and a further 20,000 of malaria, dysentery and starvation on the retreat to the Chindwin. Only around 100 prisoners were taken; the most senior officer taken alive was a captain.

Slim advanced from the Chindwin to the great Irrawaddy River. Here he showed his supreme genius for manoeuvre. Originally he had planned a direct advance on Mandalay, banking on the Japanese engaging him before he reached the Irrawaddy. But intercepts and other intelligence warned him that the Japanese intended to fight him on the Irrawaddy shore itself. While keeping up the offensive as planned, he switched his main effort 100 miles to the south. Advancing well to the west of the Irrawaddy, employing deception to cover his move, he crossed and advanced on the Japanese main base at Meiktila, 50 miles south of Mandalay and behind the Japanese. The Japanese attacked furiously, as he knew they would. Employing armour in mass, which he could do on the dusty central Burma plain, Slim utterly crushed the Japanese, destroying their Burma Area Army, which held that part of the country.

The race to beat the monsoon to Rangoon was now on. Slim had 40 days to cover between 320 and 370 miles, depending on which route he took. He chose to send a corps down each: if progress down one axis was stalled, he could punch down the other. He had to go 100 miles further than Montgomery's advance from the Rhine to the Baltic. The Japanese contested every step of the way. The axis of the 4th Corps has been described as the longest salient in the history of warfare, over four times longer than the corridor along which the British had driven to Arnhem in Holland. The advance had been at a price: the 17th Division alone lost 719 all ranks killed, 1,767 wounded and 71 missing; the Division killed over 10,000 of the enemy, capturing 211 guns and a mere 167 prisoners.

Without warning, 13 days early, the monsoon came and the advance ground to a halt. Fortunately, this had been catered for, and Rangoon fell to an amphibious and airborne attack on 3 May. At 1630 hours on 6 May the 17th Division advancing south met the 26th Division coming north, 27 miles north of Rangoon. The meeting ended one of the greatest fighting advances in the history of the British and Indian Armies.

Throughout the Burma campaign Slim had met every challenge and risen above it. He had held the show together during the grim days of the 1942 retreat, had proved a master of the grinding defensive battles of 1944, and had now shown his quality on the offensive. As an ace of manoeuvre he was the equal of Rommel, and logistically was in a different league. His proficiency in every phase of war places him way ahead of Patton, whose principal strength lay in fighting a retreating army.

In due course Slim became the Chief of the General Staff, the professional head of the British Army, and eventually Governor-General of Australia. He was Britain's greatest fighting general, bar none, since Wellington. He died in December 1970, revered by the old soldiers of his Fourteenth Army.

The SOE
M. R. D. Foot

No other armed body, except for RAF's Fighter Command in 1940, made a more important contribution to the war effort during World War II than did SOE – the Special Operations Executive.

One of the nine British secret services mobilised during the war years, SOE was founded on 22 July 1940 by a War Cabinet decision and wound up, also by a Cabinet decision, on 15 January 1946. It was created, in a tearing hurry, by Prime Minister Winston Churchill, to use back against the Nazis the dirty tricks by which (it was then wrongly thought) they had just overwhelmed Poland, France and several other states. Its task was to disrupt Nazi rule by subversion and sabotage; it worked also against Italy and Japan.

SOE was formed by amalgamating section D of the then inadmissible secret intelligence service; MI R, a sabotage sub-branch of the War Office; and Electra House, the Foreign Office's secret propaganda department. From the start it recruited rapidly: about 15,000 people passed through it. Its maximum strength, in summer 1944, was about 13,000, some 3,000 of them women. Its tooth-tail ratio was high: some 5,000 of its agents operated in enemy territory, including almost 60 women.

Politically, it came under the Chiefs of Staff, through the Minister of Economic Warfare – Hugh Dalton till February 1942, then Lord Selborne – but its existence was unknown to his office. Its propaganda section was split off in August 1941, after protracted inter-departmental squabbling, as the Political Warfare Executive, but not before its American branch had helped convince the bulk of American news media proprietors that it was better to be anti-Nazi than to be isolationist.

SOE's original chief executive, the diplomat Gladwyn Jebb, also left early in 1942. The service had three successive executive heads, codenamed CD: Sir Frank Nelson, a businessman, till May 1942; Sir Charles Hambro, also a civilian, till September 1943; and then Sir Colin Gubbins, a regular soldier with a flair for subterfuge. Its staff officers were mostly businessmen, journalists or academics, with a few regular soldiers and airmen; most of them held army officer rank; several of the most important remained civilians.

It was never a popular department in Whitehall, partly because it was new, partly because of its obsession with secrecy, and partly because it always favoured the unorthodox. Its reputation never caught up with its performance; gossip and rumour continued – and continue – to do it down. Its headquarters were in Baker Street, Marylebone; its schools, workshops and holding stations were widely scattered over England and Scotland in requisitioned country houses.

It armed its agents both with normal weapons and with ones invented to suit it, such as the cheap sten sub-machine gun, the welrod one-shot pistol (easily hidden in a sleeve),

SOE agent Violette Szabo, posthumously awarded the George Cross for her resistance work in France

the welbike (from which the modern moped derives) or the welman one-man submarine. (The last three were named after Welwyn Garden City in Hertfordshire, where they were invented.) It made much use of plastic explosive, and Colonel G. T. Rheam, who ran its main sabotage school, also in Hertfordshire, has been hailed as the inventor of modern industrial sabotage.

Several times over, SOE succeeded in inflicting damage by sabotage on the enemy war machine – in particular, by making the railways difficult for the Germans to use on the eastern front, and all but impossible on the western, in 1944. Nine Norwegians working for SOE brought the heavy water (deuterium oxide) factory at Rjukan, west of Oslo, to a standstill in November 1943, and then sank a hundredweight of its latest product in a lake, thus preventing the German nuclear scientist Werner Heisenberg from working towards an atomic bomb. SOE's private navy maintained so constant a connexion with Norway that the Norwegians called it 'the Shetland bus'.

On a wider front, SOE encouraged the formation and arming of local underground resistance groups, which undertook the task of guerrilla activity against Nazi forces in conjunction with whatever Allied invasion could be mounted. For example, even though the USSR forbade British aircraft on secret work to land in Soviet territory, it was not quite impossible to work into Poland: the Polish Home Army got enough plastic to make its mark. In Czechoslovakia, almost as remote, a two-man team succeeded in killing Reinhard Heydrich, one of the architects of the Final Solution – at a fearful price in reprisals. In France arms were supplied for over a quarter of a million resistance fighters: Supreme Allied Commander Eisenhower said resistance was worth half a dozen divisions to him. Field Marshal Maitland Wilson gave equal praise to resistance in Italy, which transcended local party differences. In Yugoslavia SOE succeeded in succouring and arming Tito's partisan resistance to the Germans, which resulted in the post-war Yugoslav People's Republic; its support was withdrawn from Mihailović's rival resistance force, because Enigma decrypts (to which SOE was not privy) showed that the Germans were much more frightened of Tito. In Greece, on the other hand, SOE kept alive a non-Communist resistance force in the mountains, in parallel with the more widespread but less actively anti-German Communist-dominated partisans. In Denmark, after a late start, important resistance forces were raised, and some invaluable special steels were smuggled out of Sweden by sea.

An efficient set of escape lines for SOE's agents ran all over Western Europe and never lost a passenger. Its best line was run by Victor Gerson, by ethnic origin a Turkish Jew. Several other Jews played distinguished parts in the field or on the staff at home.

There were disasters in the Low Countries: a deft German police operation collared all but one of the agents SOE sent into Holland from spring 1941 to spring 1943, and most of those sent into Belgium. In both cases, the disaster was retrieved in time for the advancing Allied armies to get valuable help in the autumn of 1944.

In East Asia SOE was also active. Attempts to operate in the Malay States foundered, except for the adventures of Freddie Spencer-Chapman, whose *The Jungle Is Neutral* (1963) has become a classic. Gallant canoeing parties from Australia sank some shipping off Singapore. In Burma a large paramilitary group formed by the Japanese was persuaded to change sides, and Karen tribesmen were armed to kill thousands of Japanese. Some progress was made in Siam, with august help from the Regent, and there was a small but telling SOE presence in China. Into Japan proper it was not possible to operate; just as, in Europe, SOE had hardly been able to penetrate Germany. A plot to kill Hitler, outlined in autumn 1944, was dropped, partly because of the difficulty of getting an assassin into his presence, and partly because by then he was more use to the Allies alive than dead.

The agents came from right across the social spectrum, ranging from the Regent of Siam through various princesses and noblemen to managers, peasants, railways workers and prostitutes. Most, though not all, were natives of the countries into which they worked. All were volunteers. They provided many striking examples of bravery in action, tenacity under torture, and other aspects of military endurance – though several of their achievements have become hopelessly muddled, in the public mind, with fiction (think of James Bond). Moreover, they are often confused with commandos, with the SAS, or with airborne or special marine units. Many of the most distinguished of them have left no record, either because of capture or because of the service's perpetual preoccupation with secrecy. SOE's surviving papers, now in the National Archives at Kew, include over 10,000 personal files, of varying historical value. There is very little in them about policy; in a secret service what is really secret is not written down. (W. J. M. Mackenzie's book *The Secret History of SOE* (2000), written out of interviews and archives in 1946–8 but long officially suppressed, does cover policy.)

SOE's expenses were met out of secret service funds, drawn by John Venner, its financial director, from the Treasury, and supplemented by its own efforts. These efforts were so successful, on the currency black markets in Lisbon and, still more, in Chungking, that SOE performed the unexampled feat of being shut down with its accounts in the black: it made a profit. This was due in no small part to Walter Fletcher, the son of a refugee from Austria called Fleischl, who came into SOE from the international rubber trade, failed to secure any rubber as he had hoped to do, moved on into China, and made friends and influenced people to such an extent in Chungking that he emerged with some £77 million in cash at the end of the war – much of it in US dollars.

Probably the weightiest impact of SOE was that the resistance movements it fostered gave back to countries recently conquered by the Axis a sense of national self-respect that had been forfeited by defeat – an important moral victory to place alongside the service's many strategic ones.

The Spitfire
Alfred Price

On 5 March 1936 test pilot J. 'Mutt' Summers took off from the Supermarine works airfield at Eastleigh (now Southampton Airport) for the maiden flight of the company's new F37/34 fighter. Reginald Mitchell, who gained international renown for designing the racing seaplanes that had won the Schneider Trophy a few years earlier, had produced his masterpiece.

In an age when most air forces still flew fabric-covered biplane fighters with fixed undercarriages and open cockpits, Mitchell's creation was a revelation. It was a streamlined monoplane constructed almost entirely of metal, with a retractable undercarriage and an enclosed cockpit. Power was from a Rolls-Royce Merlin Type C engine providing 990 horsepower with the promise of more to come. Early in the test programme the Vickers parent company named the fighter 'Spitfire'. By all accounts Reginald Mitchell was less than enchanted with the choice and was heard to comment: 'It's the sort of bloody silly name they would give it!'

The initial flight tests revealed a serious problem with the Spitfire, however: her maximum speed was nearly 20 mph short of the hoped-for 350 mph. That was only 15 mph faster than her main competitor for an RAF order, the larger, less advanced and somewhat cheaper Hawker Hurricane. The reason for the speed loss was traced to the type of propeller fitted to the fighter, so the company experimented with a range of different ones. Also, to reduce drag, the joints in the metal plating were filled in with plaster of Paris and rubbed down. The fighter was then painted overall in a light blue high gloss finish. Ernie Mansbridge, who directed the flight trials, later recalled:

> The new propeller was fitted on 15 May and Jeffrey [Quill] did a set of level speeds with it. When he came down he handed me the test card with a big grin and said 'I think we've got something there.' And we had, we'd got 13 mph. After correcting the figures we made the maximum speed 348 mph.

Less than two weeks later the new fighter went to the RAF test establishment at Martlesham Heath, where her excellent turn of speed and superb handling characteristics drew immediate praise from service pilots. On the strength of their recommendations, the service placed an order for 310 Spitfires.

Early in 1937 Reginald Mitchell was diagnosed with cancer, and he died in June, at the age of 42. But by then his legacy to the nation, the fastest and potentially one of the most effective fighter aircraft in the world, had proved its capabilities beyond doubt.

But further tests revealed another fault with the Spitfire: her armament of eight .303-inch machine guns was unreliable. The guns worked well enough at low and medium altitudes, but not at high altitude. In March 1937 Flight Lieutenant Dewar took the fighter to 32,000 feet for the first high altitude firing test over the North Sea. It ended in fiasco. One gun fired 171 rounds before it stopped, one fired eight, one fired four, and the remaining five guns failed to fire at all. That was bad enough, but as Dewar touched down at Martlesham Heath the shock of the landing released the breech blocks of three guns that had not fired, and each loosed off a round in the general direction of Felixstowe!

The chosen solution was to duct hot air from the aircraft's radiator to the gun bays to prevent the machine guns from freezing up. But the fighter's guns were still not functioning reliably by July 1938, and the first production aircraft delivered to the RAF lacked gun heating. The problem remained until October 1938 when, following further modifications and high altitude firing trails, all eight guns fired their full complements of ammunition. Subsequent production Spitfires incorporated the changes, and these were fitted retrospectively to earlier aircraft.

By the end of 1938 production Spitfires were emerging from the assembly hangar at Eastleigh, and the prototype's test programme was complete. That was in the days before people nursed sentimental ideas about preserving historic aircraft, and the prototype went to Farnborough for use as a 'hack' aircraft. On 4 September 1939, the day after Great Britain declared war with Germany, she suffered serious damage in a fatal landing accident. She could have been repaired, but nobody thought it worth the bother and she was scrapped. The Spitfire prototype had cost the British taxpayer £15,776. Rarely has government money been better spent.

By the outbreak of war Supermarine had delivered 306 Spitfires to the RAF, and the type equipped ten squadrons. On 1 July 1940, immediately before the opening of the Battle of Britain, Fighter Command possessed 19 squadrons of Spitfires with a total of 286 aircraft, with about half that number held in reserve to replace losses. Thirty-two squadrons of Hurricanes, with 463 aircraft, made up the rest of the modern single-seat fighter force. Of the two British fighter types the Spitfire was the faster by a sizeable margin, and only it could engage the German Messerschmitt Bf 109E on equal terms. The battle was the finest hour for RAF Fighter Command, as it was for the Spitfire. Luftwaffe aircrew unwittingly enhanced its standing further by making 'Spitfire' synonymous with 'British fighter' when reporting the cause of losses. As a result, Reginald Mitchell's little fighter established a formidable reputation with both sides.

Apart from its direct fighting role in the Battle of Britain, the Spitfire played another, less dramatic but equally important, role during that action: that of photographic reconnaissance (a function it would continue to fulfil throughout the war). About a dozen Spitfires, stripped of guns and carrying cameras and extra fuel in their place, flew daily reconnaissance missions over ports in France, Belgium and Holland, maintaining a detailed watch on the German invasion preparations. When Hitler abandoned his plan to invade, and the barges began returning to Germany, the Spitfires' photographs provided proof of the move.

Overleaf: *Mark I Spitfires flying in formation over the British coast*

Until the spring of 1942 all the Spitfire fighter squadrons had been kept back for the defence of Great Britain. But then Malta, critically important to the Allied strategy in the Mediterranean, began to suffer a ferocious aerial bombardment from the Luftwaffe as a prelude to a planned invasion by German and Italian forces. Spitfires were urgently needed to defend the island, but how could they be delivered there? The distance to Malta from the nearest airfield in friendly territory, at Gibraltar, was far beyond the fighter's maximum ferry range. Shipping crated aircraft by freighter to the besieged island was out of the question. So Spitfire fighters, modified to carry 90-gallon drop tanks, were lifted by crane onto the decks of aircraft carriers. These vessels then carried the fighters to a point about 660 miles west of the island, where they took off and flew the rest of the way. That distance, 660 miles, is as far as from London to Prague. Between March and October 1942, 385 Spitfires set out for Malta; 367 of them made it. In a series of hard-fought air battles, they first blunted the attack on the island and then helped lift the siege.

During 1942 the Royal Navy found itself without a high performance fighter type to operate from its carriers. So Supermarine produced a modified version of the Spitfire, the Seafire, with an arrester hook for deck landings and folding wings to allow stowage below decks.

Following its entry into service the Spitfire underwent a never-ending series of incremental improvements, and that process continued throughout its service life. Leading these moves was Rolls-Royce, whose engineers squeezed progressively more power from the Merlin and Griffon engines. From 990 horsepower in the Merlin Type C of 1936, to 1,470 horsepower from the Merlin 45 of 1941, to 1,560 horsepower from the Merlin 61 which entered service in 1942, to 2,015 horsepower from the Griffon 61 engine fitted in Spitfires from 1944. With each increase in power came an increase in weight, requiring the airframe to be strengthened to accommodate the changes. That long-running programme of improvements ensured that the Spitfire, and later the Seafire, remained in the forefront of piston-engined fighter design throughout the war.

Never before or since has an aircraft design been so continuously, aggressively, thoroughly and successfully developed as that of the Spitfire. Compared with the Spitfire Mark I, the Seafire Mark 47 had more than double the engine power (2350 hp compared with 950 hp). It was almost 25 per cent faster (450 mph compared with 362 mph). Its firepower was five times greater (40 pounds fired in a three-second burst, compared with 8 pounds) and its maximum take-off weight more than double (5.6 tons compared with 2.6 tons).

The Spitfire and the Seafire remained in production for 11 years. When the final Seafire Mark 47 was rolled out of the assembly hangar at South Marston near Swindon in January 1949 it was the last of just over 22,000 Spitfires and Seafires. By the end of its service life Ronald Mitchell's little fighter had equipped frontline units in 27 nations.

The tank
Brian Moynahan

On 15 September 1916, 32 rhomboid-shaped and armour-clad metal boxes moved into no-
man's-land from the British front line on the Somme. Each weighed 28 tons. They were the
largest vehicles ever to be driven by internal combustion engines. Two caterpillar tracks,
which wrapped right round their hulls, gave them a top speed of 3.7 mph. Members of the
eight-man crews fired naval six-pounder guns and machine guns from sponsons on the side.
No battlefield had seen such monsters before.

The 'tank', as the new machines were codenamed, was in secret development in Britain.
It was designed to crash through barbed wire and to provide an armoured cocoon from
which its crew could pick off enemy machine gun posts. The British commander, Field
Marshal Haig, had asked for as many as possible to be rushed over to France to try to restore
momentum to his stalled offensive on this front.

Fifty were sent. They were still mechanically unreliable, and the crews were half-trained.
Only 32 reached the start line on 15 September. A further nine broke down shortly after
moving forward. Five found themselves 'ditched', bogged down in soft ground and collapsed
trenches. Nine had engine and other defects that so slowed them down that they could only
help with mopping up. But nine of them broke clean through the German lines. The world
had caught its first glimpse of a war-changing weapon.

The tank, said to be the only real innovation of World War I, was the product of one
visionary and two brilliant engineers. These men, whose creation was, amongst much else,
to put flesh on Hitler's fantasies, were, in the eccentric British tradition, from distinctly
non-military and non-mechanical backgrounds. They were the sons of a judge, a barrister
and a stockbroker.

The idea – and the drive to see the project through – was supplied by Ernest Swinton.
He was the judge's son, born in British India in 1868. He was commissioned into the
Engineers, and a spell as an expert on fortifications at the School of Military Engineering in
Chatham was followed by a stint in South Africa during the Boer War. He had a good grasp
of the principles of defence systems, and also first-hand experience of battlefields. He was a
lively, highly readable writer. He wrote up his Boer War observations in a witty book called
The Defence of Duffer's Drift that keen young soldiers were still reading in World War II. It
advised on what not to do, as well as what tactics to adopt. His interest in future wars came
out in *The Green Curve*, a well-received series of stories he wrote in 1909.

A French ban on newspaper correspondents in the war zone led to a virtual blackout on
news of the British Expeditionary Force after it landed in France in 1914. To scotch public
anger at home, the army sent Swinton to the front as a sort of official war correspondent,

Overleaf: *Breaking the stalemate on the Western Front: the new tank in action during World War I*

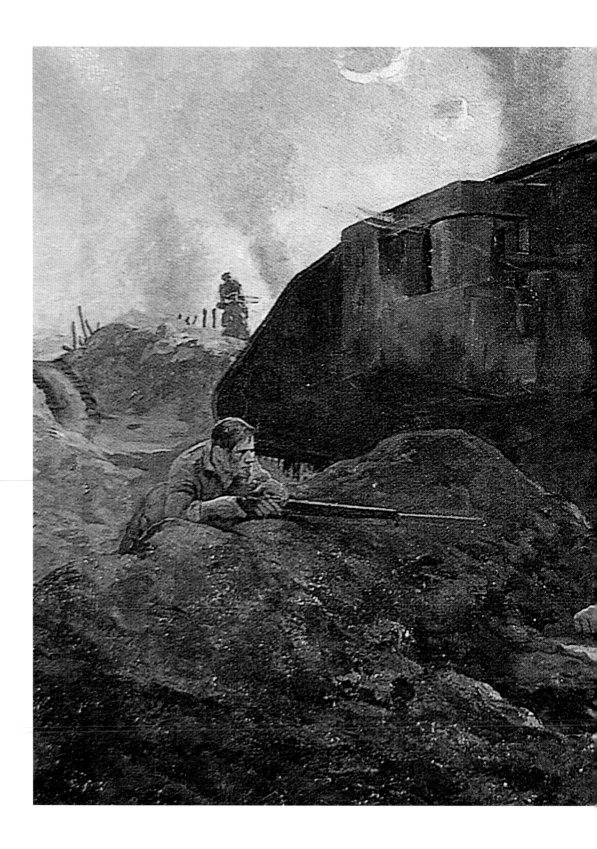

writing reports under the pen-name 'Eyewitness'. Swinton was quick to realise that the strength of defences – with three lines of trenches protected by deep dugouts, barbed wire, machine guns and rapid-firing artillery – had blunted the power of attack. The war had become a bloody stalemate.

The right mind was in the right place at the right time. Swinton thought of a solution within a few weeks. A vague notion of armoured vehicles crystallised into a definitive idea. He realised, he wrote later, that they must be capable of 'destroying machine guns, of crossing country and trenches, of breaking through entanglements, and of climbing earthworks'. Wheels bogged down easily and were vulnerable even to rifle fire: a machine with continuous caterpillar tracks would spread the weight and offer maximum traction. Pioneer manufacturers were already making caterpillar tractors.

On a brief visit back to London in October 1914, Swinton outlined his idea to a member of the Imperial Defence Committee whom he knew. He described the deadlock at the front, and how caterpillar tractors might be converted into fighting machines. The top military brass were unimpressed, but the Prime Minister was interested, and so was Winston Churchill, then First Lord of the Admiralty. Churchill, who had already used armoured cars in trench-crossing experiments, set up a 'landships' committee in February 1915.

Swinton put his proposals forward in a memorandum. The Army Engineer-in-Chief wrote caustically that, before considering them, 'we should descend from the realms of imagination to solid facts'. Nothing daunted, Swinton submitted specific requirements. The machine – the bland word 'tank' was used to camouflage its purpose – must be able to climb a parapet five feet high at a 1-in-1 gradient, cross a trench eight feet wide, and be well enough armoured to resist a reversed bullet at short range. (Bullets fired back-to-front have greater armour-piercing ability, because it is easier to stop the hard outer casing of the bullet than its lead core.)

Powerful backing came from Lloyd George as Minister of Munitions. Swinton was brought back from France in July 1915. He placed a definite contract with a tractor-maker, Foster's of Lincoln, to produce prototype machines.

These were the creation of two engineers. William Trinton, the stockbroker's offspring, was the general manager of Foster's. He worked with Walter Wilson, a Dublin barrister's boy and a design and development engineer of genius. Wilson's original ambition had been to build the world's first internal combustion engine for aircraft, and he had formed a company to do it with his friend Percy Pilcher. It was ready for testing in 1899 when Pilcher was killed flying a glider. Wilson transferred his talents to the horseless carriage, designing cars and lorries.

Trinton and Wilson's first design, 'Little Willie', was followed by the successful 'Mother' or Mark I tank. It was a rhomboidal welded box, whose caterpillar tracks went round the entire body or 'hull' – the tank was still thought of as a 'landship', and Wilson was a naval lieutenant. The sponsons, or side turrets, could carry six-pounders and machine guns. The first models had two artillery wheels for steering at the rear, but it was soon found that tanks could be steered simply by varying the speed of the tracks. The wheels disappeared.

The first Mark I was ready at the start of 1916. Swathed in tarpaulins, the secret machine was taken from Lincoln to Hatfield by train. Its trials were watched by Lloyd George, Lord Kitchener and other senior figures. Kitchener mocked it as 'a pretty mechanical toy', but the politicians were greatly impressed.

A new unit, the Heavy Branch of the Machine Gun Corps, was formed to crew the new machines; it became the Tank Corps in July 1917. Tanks were not comfortable. They were hot, and the poisonous fumes given off by the soldered joints caused crews to vomit and hallucinate; the engines burned their flesh. Bullets, though unable to penetrate the hull, could cause 'splashes' of metal from the inside of the armour to fly around like shrapnel, so that the men had to wear chain-metal face veils like ancient crusaders to protect their eyes. They could 'ditch', becoming mired in deep mud and craters, or 'belly' by getting stuck on an obstacle that brought their tracks off the ground.

Even stationary, though, they were formidable little fortresses. The crew of a tank that was ditched in no-man's-land held off repeated German attacks for two nights and almost three days. When their ammunition ran out, the crew of the tank – ironically christened Fray Bentos after the famous corned beef cans – escaped in darkness.

Just what they could achieve, in working order and used *en masse*, was made clear on 20 November 1917 when a force of 381 British tanks attacked the German front near Cambrai. There was no preliminary bombardment. The tanks broke through the wire and crossed all three German trench lines. They advanced for five miles deep into the enemy rear, tearing a hole five miles wide in the German front. They achieved this at the cost of 1,500 British casualties. Ten thousand Germans and 200 guns were captured. To celebrate the victory, the church bells were rung in London for the only time during the war. Winning the same amount of ground at Ypres without tanks took three months and 400,000 British casualties.

Tank strategy was as much a British invention as the machine itself. Lieutenant-Colonel J. F. C. Fuller, the Chief of Tank Staff, developed the classic method of tank attack at Cambrai. The tanks advanced in groups of three, with each giving the others covering fire as they pirouetted through the enemy fire-trench, his support-trench and his third-line trench. Fuller foresaw the tank being used like cavalry, driving clean through defence systems to destroy the enemy's communications and then wheeling to cut off his armies.

The Germans were late into tanks. The war was all but lost, and the British were on their Mark X, by the time the German A7V was ready, a behemoth with a crew of 16. But they caught up, and with a vengeance. The next dramatic date in the evolution of the tank was 10 May 1940, when German armour began to overwhelm France with the lightning speed of *Blitzkrieg*.

BENEATH THIS STONE RESTS THE BODY
OF A BRITISH WARRIOR
UNKNOWN BY NAME OR RANK
BROUGHT FROM FRANCE TO LIE AMONG
THE MOST ILLUSTRIOUS OF THE LAND
AND BURIED HERE ON ARMISTICE DAY
11 NOV: 1920, IN THE PRESENCE OF
HIS MAJESTY KING GEORGE V
HIS MINISTERS OF STATE
THE CHIEFS OF HIS FORCES
AND A VAST CONCOURSE OF THE NATION

THUS ARE COMMEMORATED THE MANY
MULTITUDES WHO DURING THE GREAT
WAR OF 1914-1918 GAVE THE MOST THAT
MAN CAN GIVE LIFE ITSELF
FOR GOD
FOR KING AND COUNTRY
FOR LOVED ONES HOME AND EMPIRE
FOR THE SACRED CAUSE OF JUSTICE AND
THE FREEDOM OF THE WORLD

THEY BURIED HIM AMONG THE KINGS BECAUSE HE
HAD DONE GOOD TOWARD GOD AND TOWARD
HIS HOUSE

IN CHRIST SH   MADE ALIVE

The Tomb of the Unknown Soldier
Fergus Fleming

On the eleventh hour of the eleventh day of the eleventh month of 1918, silence fell on the Western Front. Germany had signed the Armistice; the war was over; and for the first time in four years frontline combatants no longer heard the crash of heavy artillery. So complete had been the destruction that for hundreds of square miles there was scarcely a tree, bush or building standing. Towns, villages, forests and even hills had been eradicated by high explosive. From this ruined landscape the combatant nations began the long and depressing task of retrieving their dead.

During the course of the Great War more than 65 million men had been mobilised; at least 15 million of them had died and millions more had been wounded. At a conservative estimate, there was one casualty for every second of the conflict. On the Western Front, where the fighting had been most intense, the terrain was little more than an elongated burial ground. When the architect Edward Lutyens visited France in 1917 he described 'a ribbon of isolated graves like a milky way across miles of country, where men were tucked in where they fell … For miles these graves occur, from single graves to close-packed areas of thousands, on every sort of site and in every sort of position.' Of this constellation almost half a million bore British names; more than 50,000 were identifiable only as British; and somewhere in the mud lay several hundred thousand bodies whose whereabouts had yet to be discovered. It fell to Major-General Sir Fabian Ware of the Imperial War Graves Commission to sort things out.

Ware's task was overwhelming. He lacked manpower, transport and resources; such maps as existed bore no resemblance to the wasteland he encountered; the ground was littered with unexploded ordnance; apart from the battlefield graves there were more than 1,200 impromptu cemeteries in France and Belgium alone, many of which had been shelled; and he was working under severe political pressure. 'We are on the verge over here of serious trouble about the number of bodies lying out still unburied on the Somme battlefields,' he wrote. 'The soldiers … are complaining bitterly about it and the War Office has already received letters on the matter. There is every reason to expect that the question may be raised in Parliament any day.' With thousands of relatives poised to cross the Channel in search of lost husbands and sons, Ware had to provide a focal point for their grief – and he had to do so quickly. The great cemeteries at Ypres, Tyne Cot and elsewhere were far from complete, and the idea of civilians wandering through raw battlefields was untenable. His solution was the Tomb of the Unknown Soldier.

The idea had been floated as early as 1916, when an army chaplain, the Revd David Railton, saw in a French cemetery a wooden cross whose inscription read: 'An Unknown

---

For God, king and country: the Tomb of the Unknown Soldier in Westminster Abbey

British Soldier.' It struck him that a similar grave might be used as a memorial to the war dead, whether known, unknown or missing. Stripped of title, class, rank, name and number, its anonymity would represent the entire nation's sacrifice, as well as reflecting the impersonal, mechanised nature of modern warfare. The War Office was at first doubtful, but as 'numerous searching and pathetically persistent' letters flooded in, it finally gave the project its approval.

In autumn 1920 Ware's men picked through the battlefields of Aisne, the Somme, Arras and Ypres, returning with five British corpses who could be distinguished only by the colour of their uniforms. The bodies were taken on the night of 7 November to a chapel in St Pol, in northern France, where they were shrouded by Union Jacks. The following day Major-General L. J. Wyatt, commander of the British troops in France and Flanders, selected one at random. While the others were reinterred with military honours, the chosen body was placed in a coffin whose oak planks came from a tree in the royal palace of Hampton Court. Between the straps that bound it was placed a 13th-century sword that had last seen service in the Crusades. On 9 November the sarcophagus was escorted to Boulogne by French cavalrymen, at the head of a mile-long line of mourners. On the 10th, the destroyer *Verdun* carried it to Britain accompanied by six warships, and on 11 November 1920, two years to the day after the Armistice had been signed, the Unknown Soldier was placed on a gun-carriage and taken to Westminster Abbey.

London had already seen its share of commemorations, notably the victory parade of 1919, but this one was more solemn and heartfelt than any other. The cortège, led by King George V, halted at Whitehall, where a temporary plaster structure erected in 1919 had been replaced by a Lutyens-designed stone monument. The Cenotaph – from the Greek for 'empty tomb' – was a unique structure, seemingly straight-edged but in fact a mix of concave and convex curves whose subtle lines were intended to represent infinity. It bore no religious iconography, merely the flags of the armed services. The King paused to unveil it, then continued on foot to Westminster. 'Pipers marched before him,' wrote his private secretary Alan Lascelles, 'Admirals of the Fleet and Field Marshals of England on his right hand and on his left, and all London stood bare-headed as he went; while on the coffin lay the steel helmet which each one of us wore, and the long crusader's sword selected for him alone from the King's armoury.' At the Abbey a guard of valour comprising 100 men who had been awarded the Victoria Cross saw the Unknown Soldier to his final resting place. Six barrels of earth had been brought from Ypres so that he could lie in the same soil as his comrades. The King dropped a handful of the same dirt on the coffin, and then it was closed over. Like the first Cenotaph, however, the covering was temporary. It was replaced on 11 November 1921 by a black slab of Belgian granite, complete with gold lettering. The inscription read in part:

> Thus are commemorated the many
> multitudes who during the Great
> War of 1914–1918 gave the most that

man can give, life itself
For God
For king and country
For loved ones home and empire
For the sacred cause of justice and
the freedom of the world.

Together, the Cenotaph and the Tomb of the Unknown Soldier gave Britain its much-needed centre of mourning. By 14 November more than 400,000 people had visited the two memorials, and in succeeding months the number rose to more than a million. The Cenotaph would become the gathering point for future Remembrance Day ceremonies, but it was the Unknown Soldier who stirred emotions the most. As Lascelles wrote: 'Of all symbols, he is the most nameless, the most symbolic; yet few that Man has ever devised can have given such a clear cut image of reality; for every one of us who has his own dead could not fail to see that they too went with him; that after two years of waiting, we could at last lay a wreath to the memory of that great company.'

Britain's example was followed by others: France's Unknown Soldier was buried in January 1921, America's in November of the same year, Belgium's in 1922, Italy's and Romania's in 1923. (Of 3,500 US Congressional Medals of Honor only five have been awarded to foreign soldiers – the unknowns of Britain, France, Belgium, Italy and Romania.) Poland followed suit in 1925. Two years later Germany interred 20 unknowns at the East Prussian battlefield of Tannenberg, and in 1931 another was buried in Berlin. From Moscow to Baghdad and beyond, similar memorials were built – three more unknowns were later buried in America's Arlington Cemetery: one each for World War II, the Korean War and the Vietnam War – but by the end of the 20th century the concept had become redundant. In 1998 America exhumed its Vietnam unknown and, in an understandable but self-defeating spirit of inquiry, used DNA testing to give him a name. Thanks to technology, it is unlikely that there will ever again be an unknown soldier.

The black granite slab in Westminster Abbey may appear anachronistic today, celebrating as it does an empire that no longer exists and a creed of God, king and country that even then had a hollow ring. But although a monument to the dead of World War I, it is effectively a tribute to every British soldier who has fallen since, its symbolism made all the more poignant by the belief that it would be the last of its kind. The conflict it commemorated was called at the time 'the war to end all wars'. Instead it was the precursor, and arguably the cause, of others even worse.

The Victoria Cross
Bryan Perrett

It was Queen Victoria who, on learning of the numerous deeds of gallantry and self-sacrifice on the part of her seamen and soldiers during the Crimean War, provided the encouragement for a decoration to be awarded for acts of supreme courage. The award, which took her name, was created by Royal Warrant on 29 January 1856. The Warrant stated that only members of the Royal Navy and British Army who, in the presence of the enemy, had performed a signal act of valour or devotion to their country, were eligible to receive it. It also stressed that only the merit of conspicuous bravery could establish a claim for the award, and that all persons were on an equal footing in relation to eligibility for the decoration.

The Victoria Cross was, and still is, made from the metal of bronze Chinese cannon captured at Sevastopol. It takes the form of a simple Maltese cross embossed with a crown surmounted by a lion and the legend 'FOR VALOUR'. Queen Victoria made the first presentations to those who had won the award during the Crimean War at an investiture held in Hyde Park on 26 June 1857.

In total, only 1,354 Victoria Crosses have ever been awarded, of which 294 were posthumous. As its founder intended, its recipients come from every conceivable walk of life, making it the rarest and most democratic award for gallantry in the world. Great care is taken in selecting those considered eligible. This includes written statements from three witnesses to the act. In circumstances where an entire unit has distinguished itself in a heroic manner, it is awarded a number of Victoria Crosses in proportion to its size, the actual recipients being chosen by ballot among its members. The final decision rests with the sovereign, who personally presents the award at an investiture.

The circumstances giving rise to the award vary enormously. It has been won for acts of berserk fury, as in the Indian Mutiny; for acts of cold, determined courage, like that of Lieutenant Peter Roberts and Petty Officer Thomas Gould, who on 16 February 1942, north of Crete, worked for 40 minutes in the cramped space between their submarine's casing and pressure hull to free an unexploded bomb, well aware that the bomb might detonate or the boat dive if the enemy reappeared; for deliberate acts of self-sacrifice for the benefit of comrades; and for many other reasons. The greatest number of VCs awarded for a single day's fighting was 24, won on 18 November 1857 at the Second Relief of Lucknow during the Indian Mutiny. Small, desperate actions, such as that at Rorke's Drift in 1879, generated a remarkable number of VCs. Conversely, some great events that have proved to be turning points in history have produced few. For example, only one VC was awarded during the Battle of Britain, that won by Flight Lieutenant Eric Nicolson who, on the point of leaving

A pictorial calendar of 1901 honours two VCs in one family: Lord Roberts and his son Frederick

"LIKE FATHER LIKE SON."

FIELD-MARSHALL LORD ROBERTS, V.C., G.C.B., G.C.S.I., &c.

THE LATE LIEUT. THE HON. F.H.S. ROBERTS, V.C.

The Battle of Colenso. Dec 15th 1899

his burning aircraft, re-entered the cockpit to shoot down an enemy fighter that had entered his field of fire. This sole award can be explained by the fact that in the very nature of single-seater fighter combat, there will inevitably be few witnesses to individual acts. However, enormous undertaking though it was, D Day also saw only one award of the VC, to Company Sergeant-Major Stanley Hollis of the 6th Battalion The Green Howards, who single-handedly neutralised two bypassed pillboxes that were menacing his company's rear.

It can be argued that some of the acts resulting in early awards would, in more recent times, have been rewarded with a lesser decoration, but that in itself does not detract from the courage involved in their execution. Inevitably, the Victoria Cross has been earned more frequently than it has been awarded, and in some cases the award has not been made because one or more of the witnesses have been killed before the necessary statements can be made.

Over the years, the terms of the original Royal Warrant have been modified. During the Indian Mutiny the award was granted to civilians serving under military command. In 1858 the provisions were extended to include 'circumstances of extreme danger', but reverted to 'in the presence of the enemy' in 1881. In 1867 colonial forces throughout the Empire became eligible for the award. The sole exception was the Indian Army, whose supreme award for valour remained for the moment the Indian Order of Merit, instituted by the Honourable East India Company as early as 1837. Initially, no provision was made for the VC to be awarded posthumously, relatives having to be content with the phrase that the man 'would have received the Victoria Cross had he survived', contained in the despatch reporting the action. This changed during the Second Boer War when Lieutenant the Hon. Frederick Roberts, the son of Field Marshal Lord Roberts, VC, was recommended for the award following a gallant attempt to bring out a battery of guns at the Battle of Colenso in 1900. Roberts died of his wounds before the award could be confirmed, but received it posthumously, thereby establishing a precedent. Posthumous awards continued to be made, and a number were conferred retrospectively for acts that had been performed in the previous century, the principle having been approved by King Edward VII.

The original Warrant also stated that the award could be forfeited for disgraceful conduct. Eight such forfeitures were enforced for crimes varying from theft to bigamy. In 1920, at the insistence of King George V, the forfeiture clause was abandoned. In 1911 native officers and men of the Indian Army became eligible for the award, and in 1920 eligibility was further extended to include the recently formed Royal Air Force, as well as matrons, nursing sisters and nurses serving under military command.

Only three men have been awarded a Bar to their Victoria Cross: Lieutenant-Colonel Arthur Martin-Leake, Royal Army Medical Corps, Captain Noel Chavasse (posthumously), RAMC, Medical Officer of the Liverpool Scottish, and Captain Charles Upham, 20th Battalion New Zealand Expeditionary Force (The Canterbury Regiment). Curiously, Chavasse had a family connection not only with Upham, but also with Lieutenant Neville Coghill, 24th Regiment, who won the award in the aftermath of the Battle of Isandlwana. The suggestion that some sort of genetic link exists between Victoria Cross winners is obviously untenable, yet the fact remains that in three instances fathers and sons have both received the award, as in four instances have brothers, while wider family connections exist in greater numbers. The youngest winners of the VC were Hospital Apprentice Andrew Fitzgibbon and Drummer Thomas Flinn, both of whom were aged 15 years and three months at the time; the oldest recipient was Lieutenant William Raynor of the Bengal Veteran Establishment, aged 61 years and 10 months. Two awards have no name: that to the British Unknown Soldier in Westminster Abbey, who also received the Congressional Medal of Honor, the United States' supreme award for valour; and the reciprocal award to the American Unknown Soldier, buried in Arlington National Cemetery in Washington.

Since the inception of the award, members of the Royal Navy, including the Fleet Air Arm and Royal Marines, have won 119 Victoria Crosses; the British Army 837, including two Bars; the Royal Flying Corps and Royal Air Force 32; the Honourable East India Company's forces and the Indian Army 137; Australian forces 91; Canadian forces 80; New Zealand forces 22, including one Bar; South African forces 28; Newfoundland and Fijian forces and the King's African Rifles one each. Several awards have also been made to civilians serving under military command. The conflicts giving rise to the greatest number of awards were World War I, with 634 including two Bars, followed by World War II with 182, including one Bar. Since World War II the Victoria Cross has only been awarded 11 times, the most recent being made posthumously to Sergeant Ian Mackay of the 3rd Battalion The Parachute Regiment, who, during the Falklands War, sacrificed his own life to neutralise an Argentinian machine gun post so that his platoon could continue its advance.

The award of the Victoria Cross can place a heavy responsibility upon its recipients. For the rest of their lives they will be regarded with deep respect and constantly observed, so that it becomes a duty to set an example in all things, not least to the young. Those winners of the Victoria Cross whom I have had the privilege of meeting all seem to have something in common. Whatever their personalities may have been before the award was made, they all possess a quiet, modest, authoritative self-containment indicating that they have nothing to prove to anyone. Sadly, few are alive today and with each year their number grows fewer. Of course, that does not mean that the Victoria Cross will never be awarded again. The future will also contain terrifying moments of truth, and there will be those who rise to the occasion. If the history of the Victoria Cross tells us anything, it is that often they will seem to be the least likely of people.

Overleaf: *'For valour': Private Ryden outside Buckingham Palace after being invested with the VC, November 1916*

The Duke of Wellington
Jane Wellesley

By the time the 1st Duke of Wellington died in 1852 at the age of 83 he was the most famous man in Britain. One-and-a-half million people thronged the streets of London to watch his funeral cortège pass, and Queen Victoria, standing on the balcony of Buckingham Palace, wept unrestrainedly at the loss of the 'greatest man this country ever produced'. How did one who had been, in his own words, 'a dreamy, idle and shy lad', withdrawn from Eton because he was not bright enough to justify the expense, become the most celebrated of all British generals – his position on that pedestal still unassailed today?

Arthur Wesley (the family name reverted to Wellesley in 1798) was the fourth surviving child of Anglo-Irish nobility. Born in 1769, he spent his early years in Ireland, where his father was Professor of Music at Trinity College, Dublin. His family moved to England when he was 12; his father died shortly after. There followed several inglorious attempts to educate Arthur, whose only talent appeared to be an aptitude for playing the violin. His formidable mother despaired of him: 'I vow to God I don't know what I shall do with my awkward son Arthur.' Finally, he was sent to a military academy in Anjou. Within months of his return to England in 1786 he was gazetted an ensign. The seal was set.

Arthur's first posting was in 1788, as ADC to the Viceroy in Ireland. Here, however, another duty awaited him: he was expected to take his turn after his two older brothers as member for the family parliamentary seat of Trim. Soon after arriving, Arthur had a goal of his own: Kitty Pakenham, a bookish beauty who was a favourite at the viceregal court. He wooed her assiduously, but when he asked for her hand her brother, Lord Longford, summarily dismissed the proposal, considering him to be neither rich nor important enough. This rejection was probably the final spur; failure of any kind was now anathema to him. He promised Kitty that his 'mind would remain the same', but soon afterwards he burnt his violin and with it the last vestiges of the dilettante. These tumultuous personal events were happening against the backdrop of the French Revolution and the shock waves that followed it; they combined to form in him a strong distrust of change, an obsession with order.

In 1793 France declared war on Britain, and a young Corsican called Napoleon Bonaparte was given his first command. The year after, in Flanders, Arthur Wesley, by now a colonel, got his first real experience of battle, against the French. Six months later he was back in Ireland, having learnt 'what one ought not to do'. He had observed inadequate supply lines, ill-equipped soldiers and out-of-touch officers more concerned about the quality of their meals than the conditions of their men. Later in life, when asked about his success in campaigns, he replied: 'I was always on the spot – I saw everything and did everything for myself.' This hands-on approach was to prove one of his greatest strengths on the battlefield.

The future Iron Duke: Sir Arthur Wellesley, nine years before the Battle of Waterloo, by John Hoppner

He was not home for long. In 1796 he sailed for India, where he was to spend nine formative years. Before leaving he resolved to educate himself and he took with him a substantial library which included Voltaire, Rousseau, Locke, Swift and Frederick the Great. Soon after his arrival in India his eldest brother was appointed Governor-General; whatever the advantages this seemed to promise, it created jealousies which led to Arthur being displaced from a command. He minded this bitterly and it reinforced his lack of trust in others, including even his brothers. He never forgot his public duty, but hereafter it went with a private determination to 'walk alone'.

But India also gave him, amongst a string of other victories, Assaye (1803), which he always cited as the 'best' battle he ever fought. And victory gave him confidence in his judgement. He realised that discipline on the battlefield was paramount and courage was valueless without it; as he remarked, 'there is nothing so stupid as a gallant officer'. The subcontinent may have been considered a military backwater, but it gave him skills that reached beyond the armoury of warfare: he learnt to respect the religion and traditions of the native peoples and to deal with the intricacies of diplomacy.

When Sir Arthur Wellesley (as he now was) returned from India in 1805 he was a national hero, and this time when he offered his hand to Kitty it was accepted. He had honoured his promise, but his bride was no longer the young girl he had left behind; indeed, he ungallantly remarked to one of his brothers, 'By Jove she has grown ugly!' At any rate, she would never compete with his great love, the Army. She had given him two sons by 1808, when he went to fulfil his destiny in the Peninsular War: 'My die is cast, they [the French] may overwhelm me but I don't think they will out-manoeuvre me … because I am not afraid of them as everyone else seems to be.' Over the next six years all that he had learnt, briefly in Flanders and then in India, would be put to the test.

The war was not an unbroken trail of glory. There were setbacks and moments of despair: Wellesley was lambasted for signing the Convention of Cintra (1808), and morale was severely affected by the failure of the siege of Burgos (1812). But victory was the pattern: Salamanca (1812) showed him to be the master of manoeuvre, and Vitoria (1813) remains one of the greatest strategic triumphs in British history. By 1814 the French had been driven from the Iberian Peninsula and Napoleon banished to Elba.

At the start of the war Sir Arthur had been the youngest lieutenant-general in the British Army: by the end he was the Duke of Wellington and a field marshal, showered with titles, gifts and military honours. His reputation extended far beyond the boundaries of battle; for his troops his mere presence on the field was electrifying: 'we would rather see his long nose in a fight than a reinforcement of ten thousand men any day'.

'It is for you to save the world again.' With these words Tsar Alexander of Russia set the stage for the greatest and last battle Wellington would fight. In the spring of 1815 Napoleon had escaped from Elba and stolen a march on the enemy, but on the eve of Waterloo the Duke displayed his customary coolness by being guest of honour at the Duchess of Richmond's ball in Brussels: his psychological warfare required 'pleasure as usual'.

At the Battle of Waterloo the 'finger of providence' was on Wellington. But he had other things on his side; he was a consummate defensive tactician and had perfected the timing of his offensive action. His supply lines were in place, he had reconnoitred the ground, and would use his 'reverse slope' tactic (where infantry were concealed behind the crest of a hill) to brilliant effect. He inspired total confidence and, like their commander, every man on the battlefield was ready to sacrifice himself. Typically, the chateau of Hougoumont suffered wave after wave of attack from the French, but was held for the entire day by guardsmen, one of whom would later be described by the Duke as 'the bravest man at Waterloo'. When, late on Sunday 18 June 1815, Wellington left the battlefield he was utterly exhausted. He wept as he was told of the terrible losses: 50,000 lay dead or dying. 'I hope to God I have fought my last battle.' His wish was to be granted.

Wellington had finally faced and defeated the Emperor, who could claim superiority as a military commander but had misguidedly underestimated the courage and energy of the 'Sepoy General' and the constancy of the Prussians: 'this affair is nothing more serious than eating one's breakfast'. Napoleon would live to choke on these words as he spent his last six years a prisoner on St Helena.

Wellington returned to politics, evolving as one of the grandest of Tory grandees; he became Prime Minister in 1828 and held the office for nearly three years. He had many critics, but his greatest political achievement was to steer Catholic emancipation through Parliament, his Irish roots giving him unique insights into the problem. If this was his high point, the low was the Reform Bill, to which his opposition was implacable. He paid the price when his London home, Apsley House, was stoned and he was pursued by a mob who tried to drag him from his horse. His composure unruffled, he enlisted the protection of, amongst others, two Chelsea Pensioners who were passing.

The Duke continued to the end to play an active role in public life. His bittersweet relationship with his wife Kitty ended with her death in 1831, but he was consoled by the company of many clever and beautiful women, who effectively replaced his battlefield entourage of dashing young men. He was devoted to both his daughters-in-law and derived immense pleasure from his grandchildren, with whom he was playing the day before he died.

As a direct descendant, it is impossible not to feel a certain pride of association. From an unpromising beginning, Wellington's roll-call of achievements was extraordinary. By the time his coffin was lowered into the crypt at St Paul's on a bleak day in November 1852 to lie alongside that other great Napoleonic hero, Lord Nelson, he had truly earned the epithet the 'Great Duke'.

General James Wolfe
Stephen Brumwell

Late on the morning of 13 September 1759 a brief and poignant entry was made in the log of His Majesty's frigate *Lowestoft*. It read: 'At 11 was brought on board the corpse of General Wolfe.' Minutes earlier Major-General James Wolfe had been killed leading his Redcoats to victory on the Plains of Abraham, facing the French fortress of Quebec. Won against all the odds, that brief, bloody encounter had momentous consequences: it gained Canada for the British Empire and sounded the death-knell for French power in North America.

Wolfe's dramatic and unexpected victory was the highlight of Britain's *annus mirabilis* of 1759. To be sure, battles were won elsewhere around the globe, but for sheer drama nothing could match Wolfe's epic campaign on the St Lawrence. In death the 32-year-old general was transformed into the 'Hero of Quebec', widely hailed as the personification of courage, resolution, self-sacrifice and military skill.

This eulogistic interpretation lasted as long as the British Empire itself. Since its demise, Wolfe's reputation has suffered at the hands of historians; he is now more likely to be characterised as a bloodthirsty martinet, a priggish and self-centred soldier of mediocre abilities who owed his fame to a single celebrated – and extraordinarily lucky – victory. But whilst Wolfe was not the paragon of Victorian biographers, his military reputation rests upon firmer foundations than his modern detractors acknowledge.

Born at Westerham, Kent, in 1727, James Wolfe was the son, grandson and great-grandson of army officers. Keen to follow the family tradition, by 1743 he was in action at Dettingen in Germany. There, the 16-year-old lieutenant acquitted himself well as French roundshot dismembered the men around him. Wolfe's dedication, allied to his father's cash and influence, swiftly brought promotion to captain. In 1745, when the Jacobite rebellion erupted, Wolfe's regiment was recalled from Flanders; during the scrappy fight at Falkirk in January 1746 it held firm against Bonnie Prince Charlie's Highlanders. Three months later Wolfe served at Culloden. As the victorious royalists ruthlessly scoured the battlefield, he reputedly spurned the Duke of Cumberland's order to pistol a wounded Highlander: the story may have some foundation but, as Wolfe was then aide-de-camp to General Henry 'Hangman' Hawley, it's likely that *he*, not 'Butcher' Cumberland, issued the brutal directive.

Wolfe was soon back fighting the French: in July 1747, as major of brigade, he was wounded during the fierce combat at Lauffeldt, near Maastricht. It was a British defeat, but the carnage left the victors eager for peace.

By his 21st birthday James Wolfe had served five arduous campaigns and survived four bloody pitched battles. It was a gruelling apprenticeship: as he later confessed, those years stripped the bloom from his youth. They also undermined his precarious health. Throughout his adulthood Wolfe was plagued by assorted illnesses, including 'gravel' – an excruciating bladder complaint that fuelled his natural feistiness and sparked outbursts of temper.

Wolfe thrived on action, and the ensuing years of peacetime service in Scotland and England were characterised by frustration, boredom and introspective soul-searching. Increasingly, he channelled his energies into professional perfectionism. As Major, and later Lieutenant-Colonel, of the 20th Foot, Wolfe turned that battalion into a model unit. His regimental orders reveal an uncompromising disciplinarian, albeit one who showed a genuine paternalism towards his subordinates: Wolfe earned a lasting reputation as 'the officers' friend and soldiers' father'.

The peace of 1748 was merely a breather in the Anglo-French contest for global supremacy. Warfare officially resumed in 1756, with Britain suffering setbacks across the globe. In 1757 she retaliated by raiding the French coast. A projected attack on Rochefort resulted in humiliating withdrawal, but Wolfe, who served as the expedition's quartermaster-general, enhanced his reputation. When William Pitt's administration sought fresh commanders capable of stemming the dismal tide of defeat, Wolfe was named.

Promoted to brigadier-general, in 1758 Wolfe was sent across the Atlantic to join Jeffery Amherst's strike against Louisbourg, on Cape Breton. There, he commanded the risky amphibious assault that won a vital toehold on the island; his courage and energy throughout the siege left a deep impression upon officers, whose letters surfaced in newspapers on both sides of the Atlantic. Louisbourg's conquest marked a turning point in the war: from London to New York, toasts were drunk to 'Brave General Wolfe'.

The object of all this attention made an unlikely looking hero: Wolfe was tall, gangling and red-haired, with a pointed nose and receding chin. But this unpromising exterior concealed a character in which grim determination fused with fierce patriotism and vaulting ambition. Wolfe's first taste of fame left him hungry for more. Rather than spend the winter languishing in Nova Scotia, he returned to England. There, he capitalised on his celebrity by lobbying successfully for command of a proposed expedition against Quebec. The appointment of the fire-eating Wolfe to head the St Lawrence army proved popular with the rank and file: as Sergeant Ned Botwood proclaimed in a rousing ballad, those that loved fighting would soon have enough: 'Wolfe commands us, my boys; we shall give them *Hot Stuff*.'

Transported by a powerful fleet, Wolfe's taskforce reached its objective in late June 1759. Quebec was a tough nut to crack. Its defenders were numerous, well entrenched and commanded by a capable officer, the Marquis de Montcalm. Wolfe toyed with various plans before assaulting the shoreline below the city on 31 July, only to be rebuffed with heavy casualties. Stymied and frustrated, he implemented a controversial scorched-earth policy aimed at breaking the resolve of the city's defenders.

The strain of command began to take its toll. In late August Wolfe was laid low by a severe fever. Although his brigadiers had become increasingly critical of his generalship, he now invited them to 'consult' upon a future plan of operations. They urged him to

Overleaf: The Death of General Wolfe *by Benjamin West, 1771*

attack *above* Quebec, so threatening its supply line. Wolfe immediately accepted their proposal, but made a crucial modification of his own. The brigadiers wanted to land some 12 miles from the city; Wolfe decided to strike at a cove just *two* miles away.

It was a daring stratagem, and respected historians have maintained that Wolfe never expected it to succeed: dying of tuberculosis, they claim, he was prepared to sacrifice both himself and his army in a desperate, last-ditch bid for glory. But although Wolfe was ill, there is no evidence that he was dying, still less that he harboured a death wish. Engaged, and due to be married on his return, he had much to live for. Wolfe's gambit was anything but reckless. Finalised within days, the plan nonetheless reflected careful calculation of the odds: it allowed Wolfe to concentrate his troops and maximised the vital element of surprise; the night selected for the attack also exploited an unusually favourable conjunction of tide and moon.

Once he had fixed upon his course, Wolfe's leadership never faltered. Only troops with utter faith in their general could have executed what was required of them on the morning of 13 September. Passing silently down the river, they landed and scrambled up to seize the heights above. Montcalm was stunned to find a British army arrayed just a mile from the walls of Quebec, calmly awaiting attack. At Wolfe's direction, his men had loaded their muskets with two balls: the enemy were just a stone's throw away when they finally received this double dose of lead. Remorseless, disciplined volleys stopped them in their tracks. As the gunsmoke billowed away on the breeze, the Redcoats fixed bayonets and advanced over the dead and dying. It was a triumph of discipline and morale, and a vindication of Wolfe's unswerving faith in his men.

Although few knew it, Wolfe was already down and dying. Taking post on the right flank, the lanky young general offered a conspicuous target to sharpshooters. He suffered three wounds: the first, which shattered his wrist, he bound up with a handkerchief, the second and third struck him in the belly and breast. Carried bleeding from the firing line by a handful of men, James Wolfe lived just long enough to know that his bold plan had succeeded: a professional to the very last, he gasped out a final order for one regiment to cut off the enemy's retreat, then rolled over and quietly died. The Redcoat rank and file were a hard-bitten bunch, but when they heard the news many of them wept openly.

The general's gloomy final despatch to Pitt, penned on 2 September and received in London on 14 October, had offered little hope of success. Hot on its heels came tidings of Wolfe's tragic triumph: it won him the status of posthumous hero. In 1771 his fame was consolidated when Benjamin West unveiled *The Death of General Wolfe*. The painting bore little relation to reality, but bestselling engravings ensured that its depiction of Wolfe as soldier-martyr was etched upon the consciousness of Georgian Britons. For youngsters like Horatio Nelson, born in 1758, James Wolfe epitomised a new breed of officer: stern but fair, ready to lead from the front, and relentless in pursuit of his objectives. These qualities were celebrated in a popular ballad, 'Brave Wolfe': it remains a moving memorial to a great British soldier.

Biographies

Max Adams read archaeology at York and practised as a field archaeologist and teacher in England and abroad, publishing widely in academic journals. After spells as a woodsman and broadcaster, he was awarded a Winston Churchill Memorial Fellowship to research a life of Admiral Lord Collingwood, to be published in 2005. His childhood hero was Alfred the Great.

Kate Adie is the BBC's Chief News Correspondent, reporting from danger zones around the world. She is also the author of *Corsets to Camouflage*, a revelatory history of social change among women, particularly since World War I. The book was inspired by her research into the many kinds of uniform women donned as they became more and more active outside the home. It was a companion volume to an exhibition at the Imperial War Museum, of which Kate is a trustee. She is also the author of *The Kindness of Strangers*, a bestselling account of her career as a news reporter. Kate has won several awards for both broadcasting and writing and was awarded an OBE in 1993.

Max Arthur's first book, *Above All, Courage*, was an oral history of the Falklands campaign. Since then he has written oral histories of the Airborne Forces, the RAF and the Navy. His book *When This Bloody War is Over – Soldiers' Songs of the First World War* (2000) was followed by the hugely successful *Forgotten Voices of the Great War*. His most recent publications are *Symbol of Courage: A History of the Victoria Cross* and *Forgotten Voices of the Second World War*. He is the military obituary writer for the *Independent*.

Matthew Bennett is a Senior Lecturer at The Royal Military Academy, Sandhurst and a Fellow of the Royal Historical Society. He has written extensively on medieval warfare and especially the battles of the Hundred Years War during which the longbow played such a major role. He is the author of *Agincourt, 1415* (1991), the *Cambridge Atlas of Medieval Warfare* (1996, with Nicholas Hooper) and *Campaigns of the Norman Conquest* (2001).

Patrick Bishop is the author of *Fighter Boys: Saving Britain 1940*. He has been a foreign correspondent for more than 20 years.

Stephen Brumwell is a freelance writer based in Amsterdam. His books include *Redcoats: The British Soldier and War in the Americas, 1755–1763* (2002) and *White Devil: An Epic Story of Revenge from the Savage War that Inspired* The Last of the Mohicans (2004).

Major **Gordon Corrigan** was an officer of the Royal Gurkha Rifles before retiring from the Army in 1998. His last appointment was CO of the Gurkha Centre in Hampshire. Now a freelance military historian, he is the author of *Sepoys in the Trenches, the Indian Corps on the Western Front 1914–1915*; *Wellington, A Military Life*; and *Mud, Blood and Poppycock: Britain and the First World War*. A frequent broadcaster, he is a Visiting Fellow at the Joint Services Command and Staff College, a Fellow of the Royal Asiatic Society, and a member of the British Commission for Military History.

Len Deighton began his writing career with *The Ipcress File*, which became a classic film. He has written many works of fiction and non-fiction, including spy stories and war novels such as *Goodbye Mickey Mouse* and *Bomber*, and his acclaimed history of World War II *Blood, Tears* *and Folly*. He is co-author with Max Hastings of *The Battle of Britain*.

Ian Drury is Non-Fiction Publishing Director at Weidenfeld & Nicolson. He read modern history at New College, Oxford and is the author of 11 books, including histories of the Russian Front in World War II, Verdun, Jutland, the Russo-Turkish War and the American Civil War. He has edited several top-selling military partworks and was publisher of the Jane's military reference series at HarperCollins.

Sir **John Elliott** is Regius Professor Emeritus of Modern History in the University of Oxford, and an honorary Fellow of Oriel College. He has written extensively on 16th- and 17th-century Spanish and European history, and his books include *Imperial Spain, 1469–1716* and *Europe Divided, 1559–1598*.

Fergus Fleming worked in publishing for six years before becoming a full-time writer in 1991. His books include *Barrow's Boys, Killing Dragons, Ninety Degrees North* and *The Sword and the Cross*. He has also written a number of non-fiction titles for younger readers, among them Usborne's cult Newspaper Histories (in collaboration with Paul Dowswell). His most recent publication is Cassell's *Tales of Endurance*.

M. R. D. Foot was an army officer all through World War II, partly on intelligence duties; a parachutist, captured, stayed silent; later Professor of Modern History at the University of Manchester and author of a dozen books, several of them on SOE. His decorations include a Croix de Guerre and a CBE.

William Fowler has worked in journalism and publishing since 1972, specialising in military history, current affairs and defence technology. He has written over 20 books, including *The Royal Marines 1956–1982, SAS behind Enemy Lines*, and *Operation Barras: The SAS Rescue Mission Sierra Leone 2000*. A Territorial Army soldier for nearly 30 years, he served with the 7th Armoured Brigade (Desert Rats) and HQ British Forces Middle East in the First Gulf War. He is a regular broadcaster on historical and defence-related topics.

Robert Fox is a writer and journalist who has worked in southern Europe and the Middle East for much of his life. He was reporting the Falklands Conflict (1982) for the BBC when he witnessed the battle and surrender at Goose Green. He has written extensively on the Mediterranean, terrorism and organised crime. He is working on an account of the current campaign in Iraq and the role of reporters in recording history. He lives in North London with his wife Marianne Ockinga, an artist.

Adrian Greaves is a Fellow of the Royal Geographical Society and a former army officer who served with The Welch Regiment before embarking on a successful career in the Police Service. He studied the Anglo Zulu War for his PhD and is the author of a number of Zulu War books, which include his acclaimed *Rorke's Drift*. He also collects rare Zulu War medals. He and his wife devote much of their time to supporting the Zulu community at Rorke's Drift.

Nigel Hamilton, formerly Professor of Biography at De Montfort University, Leicester, is a visiting fellow in the John D. McCormack Graduate School of Policy Studies at the

University of Massachusetts, Boston. His official, three-volume biography of Field Marshal Montgomery won the Whitbread Prize for Biography and the Templer Medal for Best Contribution to Military History. He is also the author of biographies of Thomas Mann, John F. Kennedy and William Jefferson Clinton.

Robert Hardy is an actor and writer. He has appeared in numerous leading roles on stage, in the cinema and on TV, most recently playing Winston Churchill (in French) in the play *Celui qui a dit non* at the Palais des Congrès in Paris. He has been a consultant to the Mary Rose Trust since 1979, and his book *Longbow* is recognised as a standard work.

Mick Imlah is poetry editor of the *Times Literary Supplement* and co-editor of the *New Penguin Book of Scottish Verse* (2000). His own poetry publications include *The Zoologist's Bath* and *Birthmarks*. He is a Fellow of the Royal Society of Literature.

General Sir **Frank Kitson** joined the Army as a rifleman in the closing months of World War II, ending his service as Commander-in-Chief United Kingdom Land Forces in 1985. He served in Germany, Kenya, Malaya, Cyprus, Oman and Northern Ireland. He has written eight books on military subjects, three of which cover the period of the English Civil Wars, including one about Prince Rupert and *Old Ironsides*, a biography of Oliver Cromwell.

Ian Knight has written over 30 books and monographs specialising in military campaigns in 19th-century southern Africa, including *Go to Your God like a Soldier: the Victorian Soldier on Campaign*; *The Anatomy of the Zulu Army* and the

award-winning *The National Army Museum Book of the Zulu War*. In 2000 he was the historian attached to the first exploratory archaeological examination of the battlefield of Isandlwana. His television credits include *The Zulu Wars*, a three-part series for UK History channel.

Phillip Knightley is the author of ten books, including *The First Casualty*, a history of war correspondents and propaganda through the ages, and *The Eye of War*, a collection of war photographs.

Andrew Lambert is Laughton Professor of Naval History in the Department of War Studies, King's College, London. He is Honorary Secretary of the Navy Records Society, Vice President of the British Commission for Maritime History and a Fellow of the Royal Historical Society. His books include *War at Sea in the Age of Sail (1650–1850)* (2000), and *Nelson: Britannia's God of War* (2004).

Keith Lowe is a novelist, and Military History Editor at Weidenfeld & Nicolson. His first novel, *Tunnel Vision* (2001), was shortlisted for the Authors Club Prize, and has been translated into German, Swedish and Japanese. He is currently writing a narrative history of the Allied bombing of Hamburg in 1943, for publication in June 2006. He lives in North London with his partner and son.

Annabel Merullo has spent her career working in television and book publishing. She is the co-creator of the successful series of Century books, including *The Russian Century*, *The British Century* and *The Chinese Century*. She has recently edited an anthology of war reportage entitled *The Eye of War*. She is also the co-editor of *British Greats*, *British Sporting Greats* and *British Comedy Greats*.

Brian Moynahan has witnessed the still awesome sight of tanks in action as a foreign correspondent. His latest book is a biography of William Tyndale, and he is now writing *The French Century*, a history of 20th-century France – in which German panzers play an all too major role.

Robin Neillands read history at Oxford and the University of Reading. His books include *The Bomber War: Arthur Harris and the Allied Bomber Offensive*, *The Battle of Normandy, 1944* and *Eighth Army: Alamein to the Alps*. He lectures on military history at Oxford and the National Army Museum, leads battlefield tours to Europe and the USA, and is a member of the British Commission for Military History. He lives in Wiltshire and France.

Bryan Perrett served in the Royal Armoured Corps before becoming a professional writer. He has produced numerous books on military and naval history, including the bestselling *Tank Tracks to Rangoon: The Story of British Armour in Burma*; *Last Stand: Famous Battles Against the Odds*; *The Real Hornblower*; and recently *For Valour: Victoria Cross and Medal of Honor Battles*. His work has been translated into several languages.

Jimmy Perry served in the Home Guard and the Royal Artillery during World War II, then worked for 17 years in theatre and musicals before becoming a comedy writer. His writing credits include *Dad's Army* (including the signature tune 'Who Do You Think You Are Kidding, Mr Hitler?') and *It Ain't Half Hot, Mum*. His many awards include the Writers'

Guild Best Comedy Script and the Writers' Guild Lifetime Achievement Award. He received the OBE in 1978.

Alfred Price served as an aircrew officer in the RAF, where he flew with the V-Force and specialised in electronic warfare and air fighting tactics. In a military flying career spanning 15 years, he logged over 4,000 flying hours. Since 1974 he has been a full-time writer on aviation subjects and has published more than 46 books and over 200 magazine articles. He holds a PhD in history from Loughborough University and is a Fellow of the Royal Historical Society.

Andrew Roberts is a writer and historian, whose books include *The Holy Fox* (1991), *Eminent Churchillians* (1994) and *Salisbury: Victorian Titan* (1999), which won the Wolfson History Prize and the James Stern Silver Pen Award for Non-Fiction. He appears regularly on TV and radio, writes for the *Sunday Telegraph*, and is a regular contributor to the *Spectator*, *Literary Review*, *Mail on Sunday* and *Daily Telegraph*. His *Napoleon and Wellington* was published in 2001, *Hitler and Churchill: Secrets of Leadership* in 2003 and *What Might Have Been* in 2004.

Hugh Sebag-Montefiore is the author of *Enigma: the Battle for the Code*. A barrister before becoming a journalist and author, he has written for the *Sunday Times*, the *Sunday Telegraph*, the *Observer*, the *Independent on Sunday* and the *Mail on Sunday*. He is also the author of *Kings on the Catwalk*.

Dr **Gary Sheffield** MA FRHistS is Senior Lecturer at King's College, London, based at the Joint Services Command and Staff College, where he is Land Warfare Historian on the

Higher Command and Staff Course. His most recent books are *Somme 1916* (2004) and *Forgotten Victory: The First World War – Myths and Realities* (2002). He regularly broadcasts on radio and television, and writes for the national press.

Charles Spencer was educated at Eton and Magdalen College, Oxford, where he read modern history. He was a correspondent for NBC News (1986–91) and a reporter for Granada TV (1991–3). He is the author of *Althorp: The Story of an English Home* (1998); *The Spencer Family* (1999); and *Blenheim: Battle for Europe* (2004). He has also written for the *Spectator* and been a book critic for various publications. Married with five children and two stepchildren, he lives at Althorp and in London.

Julian Spilsbury studied modern history at Oxford University. After leaving the Army in 1985 he became a professional writer. He is the author of two novels, *Captain Coranto* and *Vision of the Hunter*. He also co-wrote *The Night of the Bear* with William Smethurst. His television work includes *Crossroads*, *Taggart*, *The Bill* and *Casualty*. He also writes occasional articles for the *Daily Telegraph*.

John Sweetman is the former Head of Defence and International Affairs at The Royal Military Academy, Sandhurst. He read modern history at Oxford and subsequently gained a PhD at King's College, London. His numerous articles and books include *The Dambusters Raid* and *The Dambusters*. Married with two sons, he lives in Camberley.

Major General **Julian Thompson** served for 34 years in the Royal Marines. He is Chairman of SES Strategies Plc; a consultant with Exploration Logistics Group Plc, which supports operations, including de-mining, in remote environments; and a Visiting Professor at the Department of War Studies, King's College, London. A regular broadcaster and writer on defence matters, he has published eight books, and contributed to many others.

Jane Wellesley is a TV producer. Amongst her many credits are a documentary *The Riddle of Midnight* (Channel 4) with Salman Rushdie and, more recently, *Lady Audley's Secret*, a drama for ITV. A direct descendant of the Duke of Wellington, she is currently at work on a book about her family.

Neil Wenborn is a full-time author and publishing consultant, who has written on a wide range of subjects, including British and American history and classical music. He is co-editor of the *Companion to British History* and has published biographies of Mozart, Haydn and Stravinsky. He is also the co-editor of *British Greats*, *British Sporting Greats* and *British Comedy Greats*. A collection of his prize-winning poetry has recently been published as *Firedoors*.

Acknowledgments

First published in Great Britain in 2004 by
Cassell Illustrated
A Member of Octopus Publishing Group Ltd
2–4 Heron Quays
London E14 4JP

A CIP catalogue record for this book is available from the
British Library.

ISBN 1 84403 255 8
EAN 9781844032556

Designer: Nigel Soper
Assistant Editor: Robin Douglas-Withers

Printed in China

The publisher would like to thank the following people,
museums, and photographic libraries for permission to
reproduce their material. Every care has been taken to
trace copyright holders. However, if we have omitted
anyone we apologise and shall, if informed, make
corrections in any future edition.

Page 8 Imperial War Museum (Q69593); 12–13 The
Stapleton Collection/Bridgeman Art Library; 17
Bridgeman Art Library; 20–21 Getty Images; 24 Peter
Newark's Military Pictures; 27 Imperial War Museum
(222/3130 C); 31 Bridgeman Art Library; 35 Public
Record Office; 38–39 Bridgeman Art Library; 42
Philip Mould, Historical Portraits Ltd, London/
Bridgeman Art Library; 48–49 Peter Newark's Military
Pictures; 52–53 Peter Newark's Military Pictures;
58–59 Imperial War Museum (HU 1148); 63 Art
Archive; 64 Imperial War Museum (FKD 856); 68
Getty Images; 71 Imperial War Museum (IB 283);
74–75 Peter Newark's Military Pictures; 80–81 The
Stapleton Collection/Bridgeman Art Library; 84 Kobal
Collection; 89 Peter Newark's Military Pictures; 92
Peter Newark's Military Pictures; 97 Peter Newark's
Military Pictures; 100 National Maritime Museum,
London; 104–105 © Yale Center for British Art, Paul
Mellon Collection, USA/Bridgeman Art Library;
108–109 National Portrait Gallery, London; 112–113
Mrs Albert Broom; 116–117 Peter Newark's Military
Pictures; 120 Peter Newark's Military Pictures; 125
National Library of Scotland/Bridgeman Art Library;
130–131 © Jason Askew/Adrian Greaves; 134
Bridgeman Art Library; 139 Getty Images; 142–143
Imperial War Museum (Q 32702); 146 Press
Association; 151 Imperial War Museum (SE 3310); 155
Getty Images; 160–161 © BAE SYSTEMS; 164–165
Peter Newark's Military Pictures; 168 Art Archive; 173
Peter Newark's Military Pictures; 176–177 Getty
Images; 179 published with the permission of the
Trustees of the Duke of Wellington; 184–185 Phillips
Fine Art Auctioneers, New York/Bridgeman Art
Library